A CITY SYMPHONY

Dear Dairine,

Thank you for always believing in me!

Maeve A. Dreux
x

Also by Maeve A. Devoy

The Tell Tale Collection

A CITY SYMPHONY

MAEVE A. DEVOY

TIMES PUBLISHING

Published by MAD Times Publishing

Irishtown, Lusk, Co. Dublin, Republic of Ireland
Telephone: 086 3562606
Email: maeve@mad4tales.com

All rights reserved. No portion of this book may be reproduced, stored in a retrieval system, or in any form or by any means, without permission from the publisher; nor be otherwise circulated in any form of binding or cover other than that in which it is published and without a similar condition including this condition being imposed on the subsequent publisher.

Book design by Oldtown

Cover photography by Cait Fahey

ISBN 978-1-3999-0107-9

Copyright © Maeve A. Devoy

*For my brothers
and all of the lost boys and girls*

"I frequently hear music in the heart of noise"
George Gershwin

"Turning and turning in the widening gyre
the falcon cannot hear the falconer"
W.B. Yeats

CONTENTS

Interlude Part I . . . . *page 1*

I The Voice . . . . *page 6*

Interlude Part II . . . . *page 18*

II The Bookmaker . . . . *page 21*
III The Accountant . . . . *page 35*
IV The Shopkeeper . . . . *page 47*
V The Entertainer . . . . *page 55*

Interlude Part III . . . . *page 66*

VI The Fighter . . . . *page 69*
VII The Mother . . . . *page 84*
VIII The Scientist . . . . *page 94*
IX The Homeless . . . . *page 104*

Interlude Part IV . . . . *page 116*

X The Stall . . . . *page 119*
XI The Weave . . . . *page 129*

Interlude Part V . . . . *page 141*

XII The Soldier . . . . *page 144*
XIII The Fireman . . . . *page 157*

Interlude Part VI . . . . *page 170*

INTRODUCTION

For five years or so, I lived by the Royal Canal, where I began collecting these stories, with my Dictaphone and my notebook. I wanted to paint a portrait of Dublin City.

Without the honesty and patience of those who let me interview them, I would not have been able to compile this glimpse of time. I want to thank them for their sincerity.

I have changed every name and other details to protect their identity. And as J.M. Synge once said:

"I have made this disguise to keep them from ever feeling that a too direct use had been made of their kindness, and friendship, for which I am more grateful than it is easy to say."

These stories are my interpretation of their lives.

There are also six interludes in this city's symphony, which detail pieces of my own journey, as I tried to finish this book and found myself entangled in the melody.

Maeve Aishling Devoy
2021

Interlude Pt. I

M.A.D.

2.40 PM TUESDAY, NOVEMBER 1ST

WHAT you are about to read no longer exists. Not me. Nor the city. Nor the symphony. The cobbles are covered in concrete. The paths are dripping with love locks and blood. The price of living is too much, while the worst are worth more than they ever deserved. There is no more time for deadlines. Or sitting and scratching at the cracks in lies. There is a gluttonous, coin-eyed beast slobbering and panting as it moves its slow thighs down the streets, shattering the foundation. I suggest you pay attention.

The fight has begun.

The bricks have been gathered. The memories have been stowed. The dawn has ascended, though the sky is not often blue.

The white cloths are being ripped from the tables, so go and grab your spoon. The tide is tearing the windows you cannot see through, straight from the wall.

There will be nothing left at all.

I am M.A.D.

I come from the fields of north county Dublin, where there are sharp corners, rude rodents, gas leaks and dreams of simplicity buried amongst the piling housing estates and the few dead bodies that were found. Where there are no lights shining on the warning signs. Or help for miles. Of course, I am mad; if I was not, I would not have made it out.

But that is not what this book is about.

Neither is writing pretty.

The world I have seen has its moments. They are precious. I will let them flutter in the marrow of my words and hope they vibrate within you, as they did within me.

I will not pretend the life we know is glorious.

When I moved to the city, I learnt what it meant to be a part of a community, to not be alone. I could see the road when I walked home in the dark. I could knock on a door and ask for help or a cup of sugar. I could bump into one friend or another.

I could lose myself in the hustle and bustle before the city had a new scaffolded face. No wonder nobody feels safe. Nobody knows what will disappear next.

Themselves? Or their homes?

Their livelihoods?

Or their history?

A few years ago, I was sitting in a hotel opposite the Garden of Remembrance, working as a receptionist. It was the first of November. And day eight of my ten-day shift rotation – which meant 3 pm to 11 pm, then 7 am to 3 pm the next day.

It was 2.45 pm.

The bins were crammed with wigs and witches' brooms, fake cobwebs and plastic spiders. The Halloween banners were being stripped from the mantles. The face-paint was scrubbed from the carpets. The empty bottles of vodka and rum were in orderly rows, lining the carpark wall, waiting to be recycled. The guests had all checked out, except the few lingering around the reception, dragging their heels and their heavy eyes.

I was dreary yet wired.

I had not dressed up, seen my friends or caught sight of a trick or a treat because I was sitting in the same rotting seat. Trying to snatch a sparkling or crackling of fireworks, I had perched over the desk, whenever a guest opened the door. I wished I was somewhere else.

That afternoon, I itched at the pink scarf, knotted around my neck. I dropped my hands and rolled my eyes, then looked around to make sure no one saw me.

I never felt comfortable in the navy suit uniform, with its stiff, starched edges. It was uncompromising, unflattering and unnecessary, considering what was on sale.

But who really cared?

No one really noticed me, which suited me and my dream, as I would steal a moment or two, when the guests and their problems had gone away. I would open a file I had hidden on the computer and continue planning this book, noting the questions I did not ask during my last interviews and any details I had not written down.

I made sure I used my time wisely, having noticed that it was passing far quicker than I had ever imagined. Nor had I ever imagined sitting behind that desk for three years.

Or feeling the way I did.

It was 2.55 pm.

A group of guests stepped through the door, just as the next receptionist on duty, grabbed it before it closed. I filled with relief. Then, I checked the guests in, closed my till and handed over the desk. When I ran downstairs to grab my bag, I did not think about changing out of my uniform. Or anything other than getting my bike and the hell out of there.

Back at reception, I avoided the guests and hurried out to the carpark, where I unlocked my bike and wheeled it inside. Squeezing through the crowd, I apologised and smiled, until I opened the door and bounced down the steps, gripping the handlebars of my life.

Once I was on the street, I chased the rhythm of the feet passing me by, like I was hopping from merry-go-round to merry-go-round. Looking around at the bobbing heads and listening for the charm and wonder, I heard nothing other than the drill of dizzying days, though it should not have been a surprise. As I said, I never thought I could have felt such a way.

But I should have known what was coming.

Turning left and clambering onto my bike, I peddled toward Dublin's Royal Canal, while pulling my uniform skirt down. I began to think about how I would get home and change my clothes, lie on my bed for a minute, get back up and make my way back to the canal, where there was a bonfire buried around its bend. How I would eventually excuse myself and head for the racetrack, where I would continue my interviews and pursuit of meaning and chance.

At the beginning of all this, I wanted to bring hope.

I wanted to inspire.

Then, I realised everyone was suffocating from the smoke billowing out of the struggle their lives had become. If I had not been so far gone, maybe it would not have hurt so much.

Speeding under the trees spitting crusty leaves on Summerhill, I crossed the canal and the Luke Kelly bridge. I reached my house and locked my bike to the railing, before wrestling with the lock on the front door, which was something my housemates and I ignored because we were afraid it would affect our rent. As soon as I was inside, I took that minute for myself and told myself that I had found hope, breaking against the corners of forced smiles.

A second later, the darkness destructed the metronome in my mind. I sat up, surrendering to the fact that I no longer knew what I had gotten myself into.

Or what it was all for, when I was sure that hope was no use when it was alone. And that the tick of our twisted clocks was no longer holding us tight.

That it was either the city or the people that would ignite.

I

THE VOICE

4.45 PM TUESDAY, NOVEMBER 1ST

There were red and yellow leaves trickling from the trees on a north inner city road. The wind was spinning them in rings around the cold. Darkey could not take the cracked emerald of her eyes off them. They were restless and reckless as they rode through the air, without a second to spare. They did not care what had happened there. What the newspapers said. Or whose blood was shed. They were not scared. They were dancing.

Darkey was sitting on the cushioned bay of her parents' front window, surrounded by handwritten sheets of music for her five o'clock singing student. She had been trying to finish the lesson plan when the leaves stirred her into silence.

Above them, all the windows and doors of the flats and houses were locked. The curtains were closed. The lights were off. The sirens were always wailing, while the streets, just like the leaves, were dead, along with too many of Darkey's family and friends.

Those remaining wondered who would be next.

Would things ever be the same?

"Never," Darkey said.

Shifting away from the window, her dark chestnut hair fell behind her shoulders. Her diamond shaped face was graced with a distracting beauty that rarely wrinkled with emotion.

She was looking down at the sheets of music when a car came speeding up the road. She turned to the window just as it passed by, sending the leaves into disarray.

Snapping her fingers, Darkey smirked, knowing that she would never let herself be so vulnerable. She was not raised to blow away.

She grew up in the flats across the road, where the people took care of themselves. They did not ask strangers for help. Or call the Gardai.

They hustled for everything.

Standing on the highest balconies of the flats, they would look down on the city: the banks, offices, restaurants and boutiques that paved the way to the horizon. They would convince themselves, under the clouds and the stars, that they were going to make it.

Then, they would abandon their belief, leaving it to balance on the ledge, when they looked around at bars and barbed wire confining them, reminding them of what they were expected to be: criminals, addicts and scumbags.

They were not meant to succeed.

Darkey was an only child, though she never felt like one. She was always with her cousins, sharing beds and burdens, dinners and turns pushing the pram or telling bedtime stories. She was small and easy to lose in a crowd, until she opened her mouth.

Singing from the steps of the flats, into the city and back, Darkey turned heads as she passed by; people stopped what they were doing to listen to her. To see the girl sweetening the streets with melodies that her bones seemed barely big enough to hold.

In her dreams, she was a dancer: studying in London, attending auditions and bowing before a black-tie audience. As soon as she could walk, she took classes in gymnastics, hip-hop, freeform, ballet and tap. Nobody could say no to her.

Or tell her when to sing.

She trained Monday to Friday, practiced in her spare time and competed at the weekends, when she lay in bed at night, with curling rags in her hair. She would stare at the plastic constellations stuck to her ceiling, waiting for the sound of her friends, laughing and cheering as they returned from the park or the bonfire, with the scent of soot stuck to their kisses and their clothes.

Once it was quiet again, Darkey would fall asleep, dreaming of her routine.

Looking down at the street, where the shadows were swelling, she picked up her phone and checked the time. It was five to five in the afternoon.

She was wondering where her student was, when her phone began to ring in her hand. She dropped and caught it, smiling to herself, before she saw who was calling. Sitting up and crossing her legs, she shook her head and answered.

A few seconds later, she was dragging her long black painted nails along the cushioned edge of the seat, with a look of disgust hardening her face, contradicting the compassion her voice was trying to convey. By the time she hung up, she was fuming.

Since the last drug feud shooting, she had lost two long-term singing students, not including the one that she had just lost on the phone, knowing that she could not afford to lose any more. But she could not listen to any more excuses, stained with the same tone.

She knew they were scared. That they had already made up their minds.

When they asked her to travel to them, she flinched and declined. She would not compromise her community. Or take her business somewhere else.

She would not sit there, crying over her losses either. Gathering the sheets of music around her, she stacked them into piles, while reminding herself that she was 12 years old when she first realised she would never be a professional dancer.

That she would never be good enough.

She would spend days perfecting her stance, then move onto her pirouette or arabesque. There was always something she had to correct. She was never happy with herself, no matter how often she won. She had to push herself to do better next time.

There were too many people who could not believe she had made it that far. That someone from her area had an interest in those dance classes, competitions and roles.

She laughed at them and said nothing.

They knew nothing.

By then, Darkey understood why she could not quit: they were different. She had not sabotaged any of their routines. Or believed that they could be so ignorant.

She did not lower herself by losing her temper. Instead, she kept showing up and winning, telling herself, over and over, that failure was not an option. That she had to prove them wrong.

Catching a glimpse of herself in the window, she gasped and began to fiddle with her hair, when a blue door flung open on the second floor of the flats. Two young boys charged out and down the steps, banging shoulders and cursing. The door slammed behind them.

The pigeons, loitering on the ledge, scarpered into the air.

The boys reached the bottom step, where they leapt onto the pavement, one right after the other, smooth and deliberate as a conductor's hand signalling the orchestra to render itself ready.

Darkey perked up.

Leaning forward, she pressed her forehead against the windowpane. She knew exactly where the boys were going, why they were tearing through the dead dancing leaves and racing against the gale galloping towards the coast, like they were pistons firing at the dusk and smoke.

They never let the road, or each other, out of sight, as they tightened their tracksuit bottom ties. They knew the flames would not wait. They had to make it to the Royal Canal with haste.

It was the quickest way to the bonfire.

"Fuck this," Darkey said.

****

Leaving the sheets of music behind, spilling onto the ground, Darkey walked into the hallway, put on an oversized hoody and runners, grabbed her keys and left the house. It did not matter how she looked or where she was going, there was nothing she could hide. Outside, the wind consumed her, pushing her onwards. She pulled up her hood and followed the lead. With a steady but deadly rhythm to the beat her feet were keeping on the pavement, she put her head down and kept her mouth shut. When she was ready, the words would come.

Turning a corner, she slowed down.

The shadows surrounding the orange streetlights were filled with memories she had sewn into those streets. Like sheets of armour, they protected her.

She knew the face to every bouquet, necklace and note, pinned or tied to the railings and poles. She had a story for each of them, and for each of the bereft, ridiculed and robbed.

She even had a story for the daisies that she spotted, daring to grow in the cracks of the pavements. She used to collect them for whoever was in trouble, until she got older and realised everyone was struggling. That there would never be enough daisies.

"I was never young," Darkey said.

Stopping at the side of the road, the traffic extinguished her words. She waited for the pedestrian light, then crossed and hurried over to the bridge, where she could see the sun had been slung to the roar of twilight. She glanced around, instinctively, before walking down to the edge of the Royal Canal and shivering as she let out her breath.

She used to go there every day before training. Or when the Gardai raided the flats. Or when they appeared from behind yellow tape, declaring another neighbour dead on the street.

Turning on her heel, she began to walk with the flow of the stream. She never wanted to leave her community. She was safe there, where no one judged her.

When she crossed the River Liffey, her ears popped.

Straight away, she puckered up, thinking that if people believed what they read in the newspapers, then they believed that she was up to no good. Once, she destroyed a shop's entire newspaper stand, because she knew the 'thug' in one of the headlines. Screaming her dead friend's name, she was peeled away from the destruction and escorted off the premises.

Her friend was not a criminal. But who cared? He was from the area: they were all the same.

Darkey whispered her friend's name, while toughening her pace. She knew a lot of people with addictions, convictions and mental illnesses. She never saw the difference between them and others trying to do better for themselves or their families.

They deserved to be happy.

Reaching the next bridge, she walked away from the brink of the canal and moved along the path that she knew like a vein leading straight to a beating heart. She did not miss a step. But she knew she never would. The worst thing she could do was forget where she was from.

At 18, she left to study performing arts at college in Belfast; where there were concrete floors and too many girls with eating disorders. It was a cut-throat environment in a cut-throat industry, which was just the kind of thing Darkey was used to.

She excelled in her first year.

Travelling home every weekend, to mend what the city had broken, she was faced with the fact that she had lost more than anyone else she had ever met. She filled with an impenetrable hate and an unquenchable emptiness. Then, she gave up on love, as it was more potential pain.

Sick of explaining herself, she cut herself off and showed no emotions, threw no punches and focused on her dream. She learnt from her mistakes, pushed everyone out of her way and trampled on them if she had to; it had been done to her.

"Fuck love," she said.

In her second year of college, she was done watching

her tongue. She no longer sang or cared what it took to succeed. All she could see was the failure expected of her. It was propelling her lifts, blinding her from herself, while the poor college facilities were giving her injuries.

She was walking up the stairs, on her way to the Christmas ballet rehearsal, limping with shin splints, when a bone in her leg fractured. There was silence, except for the crack that shattered her dreams, left the students around her gasping, tiptoeing away, knowing that she would never dance professionally again. Darkey knew it too. But she held onto her tears, until she was alone.

Emerging at the top of the bridge, the wind tore off her hood and swung the sweet scent of soot at her. She stood still to breathe it in.

The sound of pebbles grinding against the dirt behind her startled her. She turned around and surveyed the path, noticing a young boy on a red tricycle, stitching himself to the stone wall and wrapping himself in the shadows. She continued to look around, pretending she did not see him.

He did not move.

Darkey did.

****

Picking up a pebble, Darkey tossed it down the pavement. The boy stiffened and stared at the ground. He was wearing a red hoodie with the frayed hood pulled up and his mousey brown hair sticking out in tufts. His cheeks were freckled and speckled with dirt, just as his hands were. Darkey had not seen his eyes because he had not looked up. He did not know Darkey was playing his game. Or that she knew who he was, though she rarely remembered his name as often as she saw him peddling around the streets. If she had seen him earlier, she would have told him how to get to the bonfire.

Fortunately, he already knew.

A gust of fiery air came and ruffled Darkey with its smoky fingers. She spun around and smiled, while looking up at the wispy clouded night.

"I was never young," she said.

Eyeing the journey ahead, she crossed the road when the traffic cleared. She found a melody rippling from the sole of her shoe, through her limbs and her lungs.

She stood by the other side of the bridge, lifted her hands and searched the wind for the notes she needed. Then, she played the keys and began to sing.

The lyrics rising from her tongue were words she thought she could not write because she never sang about her life. In that moment, she knew it was time.

Walking as smoothly as she sounded, she swooned and took a left.

When she injured her leg, she was helpless. She continued to go to classes for two weeks on crutches. That was how long she could stand the torture.

Then, she packed up her stuff and went home.

In the midst of blaming everything and everyone else, she realised she had sabotaged herself. She never listened to anyone else. Not even to the doctor who told her to rest her leg the first time she got shin splints. Her entire focus rested on her competition.

With nowhere to go, and nothing to do, she had to sit by that window, dissecting every decision that she had ever made. She went through her old notebooks out of boredom. She opened boxes full of pictures, trophies, medals and mementos from those she had lost. Amongst the memories she had buried with the hurt, she found herself.

Then, everything made sense.

For years her mother had been begging her to quit dancing. To sing instead. She would record Darkey singing in the shower and play it back to her, over and over. Darkey would tell her to leave it alone. That it did not matter how happy it made her: she had to train.

By the time her leg healed, Darkey had changed.

She was teaching dance classes in the community centre near her grandmother's house, where Darkey's parents moved when her grandmother passed away. Darkey remembered the day they lost her like it was yesterday. And what she would always say to Darkey: *Never hold back. Sing your heart out.*

Darkey always swore that she would.

After buying a cheap guitar, she took some singing lessons. She quit running from the pain and sat with it, knowing that if she understood it, she could find a way to use it.

Beginning the following September, she moved to Liverpool to study music. She did not return for four years, until she had a degree, countless performances, collaborations, finished scores and future projects. The singing lessons were her bread and butter.

They were far, far from her dream.

Arriving at the end of the path, she let the melody fade from her mouth, while taking a look around, making sure she was alone. Then, she disappeared through a fence, scaled down the dirt and stones, and followed the glow of the streetlights, floating like lanterns along the canal's surface. She stepped under the stone arches, into the pitch black, without batting an eyelash.

When she was beside the rusted railway track, she sped up. The track had been out of service for as long as she could remember. It had been a cemetery for cigarette butts, crushed cans, hearts and morale. It was a constant reminder of why she had to make it.

Throwing her hood up and her head down, she stepped out from the arch and strode towards the blazing crown of the city, where her family, neighbours and friends were gathered, chatting and arguing over who had the best chance of winning the lotto.

The children were chasing each other, lighting sparklers from the flames of the bonfire.

"I was never young," Darkey said.

"But I am not yet old."

She began to sing her new melody, as a train chugging on the air in the distance, rattled the railway tracks like violin strings. The wheels beat a rhythm on the iron beneath them.

The crows lurching from the electrical cables, squawked and clapped their wings.

Darkey stopped still.

For an instant, she believed it was the beginning of the city's symphony. That it must have been what the leaves were dancing to earlier.

Then, she heard a familiar tune, chiming over the crackling bonfire. She looked up and saw the crowd, arm-in-arm, swaying and harmonising.

She took a few steps closer.

Recognising the song, she started laughing and running toward them. She had co-written the track with a band in England. It was all over the radio. All over the world.

She reached the singing mob and embraced them as they closed in around her, hugging her. She sang with them, noticing her mother, who had seen Darkey's work all over the ground at home and had known exactly what had happened.

And exactly where to go.

Where there were no lights, and not too many people travelled by, Darkey's community – her family, friends and neighbours – took the last of the wood, scrap and tyres, which the children had been collecting and competing for all year. They spent the day stacking the bonfire base. Then, the entire evening watching it burn.

Together, they stood, purging anything that was holding them back. They celebrated how far they had come, remembering the reason they were all there.

They were survivors.

Darkey looked around at them, smiling with pride. She turned to her mother, who was teaching the children Darkey's song, though she could not sing.

She owned an alterations business and designed the outfits Darkey needed for her performances. She was Darkey's biggest fan. And her best friend.

Her father was still at work.

Walking over to the flames, Darkey warmed her hands, knowing she had to get home and back to work. She began thinking about the melody she had been singing, and where the notes would rest on the stave, when the wind came and tightened the tips of blaze, revealing the boy on his tricycle, pedaling along the edge of the light and smiling

Darkey laughed and shook her head, before preparing to say her goodbyes. She inhaled the smoke and the legacy entwined. She did not realise the fire was reflected in her eyes.

"I was never young," Darkey said.

"But I am not yet old."

Interlude Pt. II

M.A.D.

6.15 PM TUESDAY, NOVEMBER 1ST

Something was brewing beyond the bend in the Royal Canal. Something far greater than the thrashing bonfire, spitting splinters like sizzling glitter. There was no way to deny it. Or perfectly describe it, other than a cauldron bubbling with the hearts of the community, spilling smoke that was both blinding and binding. I walked away with my eyes and skin burning, imagining I was carving a dark silhouette into the flames, cauterising myself into the flesh of the city. I stepped into the blackness, knowing the balance was shifting.

Following the rippling light along the canal, I tripped over mud-covered stones and the bones of what had been abandoned there. The chilling wind prickled the hairs on my neck, though the warmth I felt from the welcome earlier was charging my step.

I hurried up and smiled.

When I was a child, my parents would drive me to a different housing estate every Halloween, just so I could go trick-or-treating. Or watch the firework display.

I would have to say that I was from around the corner, just

so I could partake, then escape in the binbags I had fashioned my costume from. This time, it was different.

The words were not a lie.

Approaching the bridge over the Royal Canal, I veered left and skimmed through a steel fence. I walked up to North Strand, where the city beeped back into existence.

I crossed the bridge and the street stuffed with traffic, brimming with the belief that I belonged, until I noticed the stares. Everywhere I looked, the people passing me by, were looking at me as if I had risen from the bonfire, scorched and scarred.

Maybe, I was being paranoid. Or maybe, I was wrong. Maybe, I did not belong.

Either way, the looks did not stop.

Quickening my pace, I stripped the solace from my face and replaced it with a leaden gaze. I reminded myself that I lived just around the corner. That it would not be long before I was out of sight. I was losing grip of the shredded sense in my mind.

As I said, it was almost gone.

Turning left, I stole as many inches ahead as I possibly could, while the eyes wearing me down, began to look around at each other for an explanation. Or some sort of validation.

I could not take it.

Without a way to swerve the torrents tormenting me, I headed straight for the road, separating me and the flats that flanked the Tolka River. The colour of the traffic lights did not matter. Nor did the surge of speeding cars. There was only a deafening urgency to bash the heads of the clocks, binging and bonging in my chest. Until there was not.

The silence surprised me, stopping me in my tracks.

A breath later, the pain was unmatched.

It bore into my ankle, tearing me down to the pavement, where the crash and scratch of metal accompanied me. Scowling, I lifted my head, noticing a young boy sprawled out beside me, glaring at me like I had broken the rules of the game.

Jumping up, he picked up his red tricycle.

"I'm sorry," I said.

I stood up.

The pedestrian light turned green, ringing across the steam of the waiting cars. The boy leapt onto his tricycle, trying to peddle away; but the chain-guard was cracked and bent out of shape. Kicking it swiftly, he tried again.

Then, the tricycle took off, tick-tick-ticking.

The boy peddled and bounced onto the road, manoeuvred by the bumpers, curved onto the path and into the flats. The lights changed. The cars moved and swapped lanes.

I dusted the graze on my ankle.

Smelling the smoke on my clothes, I decided to leave my bike at home. I swung around and spurred myself toward the city, toward the racetrack and the meaning of chance.

II

THE BOOKMAKER

6.30 PM TUESDAY, NOVEMBER 1ST

EVERYONE WANTS to be a winner. To have the opportunity to predict the future. To place a bet, or take a bet, and know they were right. That the stars had aligned just for them. If they did not, Louis would be out of business. He calculated the odds and the dogs raced. It was an old game. But it was a good one. And he had been playing it long enough to know that for punters to put their money down, he had to give them a taste of what they wanted.

In the hallway mirror, he checked himself from every angle. His tailored suit hung handsomely. His silver hair combed back perfectly. His watch glimmered. Nothing, it seemed, was out of place, until he smiled.

Then, the nerve below his right eye trembled.

He dropped the act and grabbed his car keys. The pleasantries were not a necessity. But getting to work on time was. Stepping outside, he locked the door behind him.

The two-storey detached house dominated the darkness around him. He crossed the concrete to his Mercedes, hopped in, buckled up and took off into the mountains, down the winding road that led to the motorway.

He did not look back.

He had an hour to collect his father and get to the track before betting began. He reached over to the passenger seat, grabbed that night's racecard and balanced it on the dash.

Reciting the odds he had scribbled down that morning at the race meeting, he stalled on the dog that had taken his breath away: She-Ra was her name.

She was a stayer.

Pure white with pink paws, she never faltered in form or lost. She was an impeccable dog. Louis could not deny it. He had put his money on her, more times than not.

Then, she disappeared from the racecard. That was two years ago.

When he saw her name earlier, he was surprised. She was racing alongside two young dogs that had been winning recently.

She was too old, he thought.

20/1.

The numbers were traced, over and over, in black ink beside her name. Those odds would reel the punters in, for a look if nothing else; it would set their blood racing, which was exactly what Louis wanted. He sat back and accelerated.

The dogs were all that mattered for the next few hours: he needed a level head. He pulled a Marlboro Red cigarette from his shirt pocket, sparked it and rolled down the window. The wind sliced through the car, cutting away any comfort.

He had never dreamt of being a bookmaker. A pilot, maybe. A racing car driver, maybe.

Never a fourth generation bookmaker, hoping that he looked the part. That he had taken the gamble out of gambling.

At 54, he believed it was too late to change.

needabortionireland.org

089 490 2517

TEXT ONLY
6PM - 9PM

He had no qualifications. No other work experience.

There were deep lines carved around his eyes, which was what he got for spending a lifetime beside the track. As a young boy, he worked for his father and his grandfather, running up and down the bookmaking line, keeping track of their competition's odds.

He was always the quickest to do it too. But everyone knew that Louis enjoyed a bit of friendly competition. In school, he played poker instead of going to class, reckoning that it did not matter, once he won.

He tried the suit and tie, nine-to-five job when he was 17: he went to work in an office and quit two days later. He could not hack the pace.

His father was not surprised. He told Louis it was time for him to join the family business. He had to start earning some money.

Louis agreed with him.

At 19, he was the youngest person to ever apply for a bookmaking licence. The Gardai forced him to find a guarantor. His father obliged without any hesitation.

Louis had seen a lot of guys go bust: the money was not coming in, so they could not pay back their borrowings. Other guys walked away because they were losing. They could not see how it would ever work out. Either way, they were left with nothing.

Louis went into it with his eyes open.

There was one track, 12 races, four nights a week to be exact; the races were every 12-14 minutes, which left the betting time at four to five minutes. When the money comes in, the dogs go out and the odds fluctuate. It was easy enough, once he got the hang of it.

Most importantly, Louis understood he had signed up for a life with no guarantees. And no one else to blame.

Take the traffic lights just up ahead, turning from amber to red at the edge of the city.

"Will I make it?" Louis asked.

"Will I take the chance?"

Every young fella has a heavy foot – try telling them to come back tomorrow. That there was no such thing as the last race. They will not listen to it.

Louis did not.

He thought he knew it all in the beginning. That his father and his grandfather were outdated. Then, he went belly up, just a few weeks after going out on his own.

He had nothing.

Speeding toward the changing light, he gritted his teeth as the adrenalin shackled the breath that was charging through his chest. He eased off the accelerator and exhaled.

That was what bookmaking was all about: weighing up the odds. They were all a bookmaker had in his favour. Stopped at the red light, he lit another cigarette.

He was an old dog. He did not need to win every race.

****

Parked outside his father's house, Louis kept the car running and beeped the horn. There had been more traffic in the city than he had expected. He was running late. Checking his face in the rear-view mirror, he cracked another smile that made him shiver and look away. He picked up the racecard and began to tap the steering wheel. His eyes were darting from the odds to the car clock. He stopped and undid the top button of his crisp white shirt.

He was at the top of his game. He had nothing to worry about.

"Are you ever going to give those cigarettes up?" his father, Louis. Snr., asked. "The smell off them!"

Louis jumped.

His father lowered himself into the passenger seat, shut the door and buckled his seatbelt. He turned to look at Louis, who was looking at him, when a set of passing headlights poured over the car's windscreen, filling the space between them and defining their likeness, their pressed suits and ties, their cool and hardened eyes.

Once they put their tweed caps on straight, they turned away.

"You're wrong about that one, son," his father said.

He was pointing a wrinkled finger at the 20/1, written beside She-Ra's name. Louis shook his head and pulled off.

"It's nice to see you too," Louis said.

They laughed.

That was not the end of it though. As Louis drove towards the racetrack, his father reminded him that he had learnt from the best. That even as a young boy, charging up and down the track, he would have known better.

Or at least, he should have.

"What are you thinking? Of course, an old dog can win!" his father exclaimed.

Louis agreed.

But his father did not know She-Ra the way he did. Louis was being reasonable: the other dogs were stronger.

"Give it a rest, please," Louis said.

Then, there was silence, except for the city, shining like honeycomb around them, humming like muffled bees. It reminded Louis of the arguments his parents used to have;

how they would shut their bedroom door, lower their angry voices and come back out, laughing and blushing at each other.

They were always kind to each other.

They raised four children and bought a bigger house, a better car, when they could afford to. The trick to it, his father had taught him, was to leave the business at the track. He never took it home. Or took his frustration out on others.

He never spoke of winning either. He either broke even or lost.

Eventually, Louis's mother stopped asking.

Louis met his wife, Anna, when he was 21. He was on holiday with friends in Portugal, when he spotted her dancing alone at a bar. He would not leave without getting her name, or without learning that she was 20, from Spain and working there for the summer.

Six weeks later, Louis was still there, where he proposed to Anna and she said yes. He had never been more sure of a bet.

With her dark hair and feisty charm, Anna made him believe for the first time that there was such a thing as luck. He knew that was something special.

Louis's father had to call and ask if he planned to come back to work.

Their time was up.

They moved back to Dublin, raised three children, bought a bigger house and car. They had everything that people wanted, except time together.

Louis was working almost every night of the week, every holiday and long weekends. He was never around. Or able to attend any of the family gatherings.

If he wanted to make a living out of bookmaking, he had to be standing by the track, watching the dogs. It was that simple.

He could not afford excuses.

Or illnesses.

Most people assume the bookmaker always wins. But he does not. He has bad days, weeks and months. There was no telling when it could all go wrong.

Bookmaking was a slippery pole. It had no memory. No favourites.

He had to be nice to people on the way up because he would be meeting them on the way down. It was not a matter of maybe, but when.

At first, Anna understood; but after 23 years of marriage, why could Louis not take more time off? Why did she have to do everything on her own?

Louis tried to follow his father's advice, but by the time the children were grown, the arguments were over. They were at a dead end.

They had lost sight of each other, trying to protect themselves. And for the first time, Louis could not tell what Anna was thinking. Or who she would put her money on.

"You alright there, son?" his father asked.

Louis jolted upright.

The stadium was just up ahead, bleaching the night with its fluorescent lights. He tightened his grip on the wheel, then turned into the track carpark, rolled up his window and parked beside the entrance, where security had designated a spot, to save his father a longer walk.

"Yeah," Louis said. "I'm grand."

And as he picked up the racecard, he dropped the thought of his wife.

****

Inside the stadium, everything changed. Time moved faster. Everything got louder. Even the crowds of family and friends were in a fiendish frenzy, dictated by where the money was going. Or rather, on which dog. It was as if nothing else lay beyond the stench of opportunity and stale beer. It was infectious. Louis could not deny it.

The buzz never got old.

It was the reason he never hung around after the meeting. The only thing that remained the same was Louis. With him, what you saw was what you got.

It was called fixed odds.

The better bet.

Louis walked ahead to open the track door for his father, who held Louis's arm, closing the door behind them. In front, the track lay quiet and untouched. Louis took a moment to savour how it looked before the mayhem of winners and losers erupted.

It was peaceful.

Pulling a cigarette from his coat pocket, Louis lit it and exhaled. The smoke clouded around him, then swooshed away with the wind, just as the stars abandoned their robes and the moon spied all below it.

He reminded himself, as he always did before taking any bets, that luck had nothing to do with his odds. Dropping his cigarette and squashing it, he tightened his coat collar, put on his leather gloves and walked toward his spot at the top of the bookmakers' line.

Thinking back on the time he had spent at the bottom, working his way up, a smile crossed his lips. There were only a few bookmakers left, so it was not much of a line. But that did not matter to Louis. He was exactly where he was supposed to be.

His father was already seated in his fold-out chair beside Louis's board. He was waving his watch at Louis, who liked to do his own parade before the races began.

"Nothing gets by you father, does it?" Louis said.

They laughed.

Louis patted his father's shoulder, then took off into the stands. With his race-card in hand, he moved without hesitation, and was greeted with warm smiles and easy laughter.

Anywhere else, it would have looked like friendship. Beside the track, it could only be about two things: the dogs or the cash.

After his lap, he returned to his board, where his runner, Matt, was waiting. He was an old friend, who had been a bookmaker for a season or two back in the day; but it did not work out for him. Louis liked him. He was great at his job.

When he filled Louis in on his rival's odds, he did not mention anything about She-Ra. And Louis did not have time to ask. The stands were filling up. The lure was pacing.

Louis checked his watch and took out a cigarette. He would do well if he kept a cool head, which was easier said than done, when everything was falling apart.

Putting the cigarette away, he took a deep breath.

The first race was always the worst.

He examined the first group of dogs to be walked on the track's podium. Then, stepping over to his board, he stuck out his neck and furrowed his brow.

As the dogs were paraded, he inspected each one carefully. He did not display any odds, until he was certain he had priced them correctly.

"Here we go," his father said. "Watch out!"

A small crowd of punters descended from the stands. Louis stood with his hands in his coat pockets, facing them, ready to take their bets.

He smiled and moved amongst them effortlessly, charming them, taking their betting slips, cracking jokes and laughing while folding their cash. When the signal triggered, he stopped taking bets. He turned to face the track, just as the lure passed.

He froze.

The traps went up and the dogs charged out. Louis stood still, preparing himself for the worst. Even after laying the whole race, he did not smile or celebrate. He cleared his throat, then his board, paced the track wall and went over his numbers.

By the third race, his punting line was longer and thicker. He had to work quicker to keep track of the money, to place the dogs and take a breath.

The other bookmakers were not doing as well. But that did not surprise him. They kept going inside to keep warm. That was their first mistake.

Louis had not budged. He smoked a cigarette whenever he could. But that was it.

Before he knew it, it was the ninth race. He was staring at the 20/1 shot, pondering what could go wrong, when She-Ra appeared on the platform. Louis took a step back.

She-Ra had barely aged a day.

Wearing the red number six, she stood beside her trainer and her competitors, in front of the shivering, swaying crowd, without turning her head or making a sound. Whether she was focused or tired, he could not tell. He examined the other dogs, then put up his odds.

She-Ra: 16/1.

Another queue started to form, full of rosy faces and questions about the 16/1. When betting time was over and the dogs were in their traps, there were only two bets, each of a fiver, placed on She-Ra. It was no shock to Louis, who got exactly what he wanted.

Bang!

The dogs were out.

Dog two, dog three and dog four were fighting for first. Dog one and dog five were tight behind them. She-Ra was on the outer edge, last but strong.

The first corner was a tight fit. The other dogs were too close. They were butting heads as they grappled with each other. The crowd was fixated on every bit of dirt that was kicked back on the track.

At the second corner, dog three slipped and went down and over his head. The other dogs went down with him. It was She-Ra who shot by, straight through to the finish line.

The crowd erupted.

Louis howled.

It was a guttural sound, like a wolf that had gone too long without crossing the moon. It made him laugh momentarily.

His mask slipped.

He took off his cap to fan his face, while the other dogs picked themselves up. Louis's father patted him on the back, then sat down.

"She did it," his father said.

But Louis barely heard him. He was looking from the track to the stands and back, slapping his hat off his leg. He knew he had gambled.

He had been lucky.

"She had a little help," Louis said.

When he fixed his hair and straightened his cap, the bookmaker was back. Once his odds for the next race were up, so was the queue.

****

All debts settled, Louis could go home. His father was waiting for him, asleep in the car. Louis smiled with relief to see him. Since his mother died seven years ago, his father had not missed a night at the track: he was still sharp as a tack. Louis opened the car door and threw his stuff on the back seat, then eased himself in, reversed and pulled off. The stadium lights shut down behind them, darkening the city.

Wishing the track would not follow him home, he rolled down the window and lit another smoke. It was not time for a post-mortem. Not yet.

His father slept until they turned onto his street, where Louis could see the tip of a bonfire, burning beyond the rooftops, ripping the shade from the pleats of housing like a sheet. He pulled to a stop, waking his father, whose head bounced up with heavy eyes.

"Are you sure you're alright, son?" his father asked.

Louis laughed.

The seatbelt held his father up as he leaned forward, grasping his cap firmly between his hands. Noticing the hallway light that his father had left on, Louis reached across and lay a hand on his chest, then unbuckled him.

He was alright, Louis thought.

They both were.

They hugged and said goodbye, with the smoke from the bonfire bringing them back to life. Once his father was inside, Louis drove off, out of the city and back to the motorway, where the crystal lit night was laid out like loot on dark velvet. And where the dogs were no longer there to distract him, but to haunt him.

He turned on the radio.

Frank Sinatra's "That's Life" came crackling out. Louis turned up the volume and sang along. He let his mind travel back to 1983, when he was clerking for one of Ireland's greatest bookmakers, Billy Staunton, who wore a pin striped suit and fedora hat.

He dealt the cards at The World Poker Tournament in Las Vegas. Louis travelled with him as a clerk. He got to see the best players of that time playing one of his favourite games. Then, he saw Frank Sinatra perform.

How could he ever forget it?

He was born for it.

Driving up the winding road to his house, he parked and turned the engine off. The pitch black painted over him. The city twinkled behind him.

He grabbed his things and stepped out of the car. He had not left any lights on. He could hardly see the thirsty plants bashing their heads against the windows and the walls. Since Anna left three weeks ago, everything had changed, except Louis.

Walking inside, he turned on every light, threw his things by the door and walked into the living room. After pouring himself a glass of whiskey, he sat down and took a long swig, before trying to think about what he had done wrong.

He focused on the silence, confining the tiny tick of the expensive watch that entwined his wrist. Echoing through his life, somehow it no longer seemed to fit, along with the house that was now too big and the lawn that was far too long.

His wedding ring began to itch his skin, so he took it off and placed it on an empty coffee table. The only thing that felt right was his suit.

Why would he change?

He made himself comfortable, then sipped his drink. The race-card peeked out of his top pocket. The 20/1 was the perfect shot at the old dog's heart.

He sat there with all the lights on, knowing the only thing he could depend on, was if there was money to be made at the track, he would be there calculating the odds. As any old bookmaker would say, he did not have to win them all.

He fell asleep in the chair, holding his glass, with the last drop left to drink.

III

THE ACCOUNTANT

0.00 PM WEDNESDAY, NOVEMBER 2ND

At the stroke of midnight, a group of men in suits walked out of The Quays lap dancing club. They wore woozy smiles and loose ties. They had just bought eight dances off Viola. That put her at ten so far that night. A few more and she might smile. Sitting on a velvet sofa, wearing red laced lingerie and thigh high stockings, she scanned the floor of the club with her cruel, blue eyes, calculating the potential profit. Minutes were money when she worked there.

Deciding to wait, she heaved her buxom like bait. Her belly button ring glittered in the dimmed light. Her dyed blonde hair had dark roots and ironed tips that curled against her pale shoulders. There were stretch marks lining her stomach. There was nothing she could do about them. If men did not like her, they could go somewhere else.

"They'll come crawling," she said.

"They always do."

Two girls were working the stained red carpet. The younger was chatting with two men at a table. The other was slinking around the silver strip pole. Viola cringed as she caught a glimpse of her. She was reminded of why she never went near the pole.

There was no money in it. And unless the dancer could do the splits upside down, it put the punters off. Viola preferred to stick to what she was good at: counting.

Each dance was three minutes long. It cost €30, which meant €10 a minute. The dances were paid for at the reception to the dance parlour upstairs, where the profit from her first dance always went to the house. Everything after that, went into her pocket.

Lap dancing was legal and safe. The cash was untraceable: no records were kept. The money was worth it, if the women were able for it.

Despite what people believed, none of the women were forced to work there, or in any other club she had worked. They were all there for the same thing.

Viola had met only one dancer whose boyfriend made her dance. All she did was cry on the club floor. She made nothing. Viola and the other dancers paid her airfare home to her mother in Romania. They stuck together that way. But not in any other.

There were rules, just like any job. They could not take their G-strings off. Or let the men touch them. Some dancers let men grope them, which gave the men the wrong idea.

Viola complained about it once. But her boss laughed at her. Those dancers were making more money than she was. He could not see a problem.

When she started dancing four years ago, she was 23 years old. She sat at the back of the club drinking, shaking and avoiding the men. Eventually, one of the older dancers approached her, telling Viola to come with her.

"You have to make money," the woman warned. "The boss is watching."

Walking over to a table of two Indian men, the woman sat down and started talking. Viola followed her lead. She could barely breathe because of her nerves. Or maybe she had drunk too much alcohol. Either way, she did not say a word.

A few minutes later, the son bought his father a dance from each of the women. The older woman stood up and winked at Viola, before paving the way to the dance parlour, where she performed first so Viola could see what she had to do.

It was the only bit of help Viola ever got.

Taking her clothes off was the easy part. Getting money out of the men was hard. They had to be told that it was ok for them to be there. That their wives and girlfriends had nothing to worry about. They were not swapping numbers or having sex, so they were not cheating.

The glare seizing Viola's stare was real: she despised the men, though she usually disguised it. Some of them liked it, which did not surprise her. Nothing surprised her anymore. Only her ability to assess and adapt.

She bent over to pick up a champagne glass on the table, spilling just enough cleavage to turn some eyes. Her glass was filled with lemonade and sparkling water: it was called a Dazzler. The dancers got a commission for each one a customer bought them.

Viola drank nothing else.

Swallowing her last sup, a man stood up at the bar. She pulled up her stockings, then looked in the opposite direction. She had spotted his wedding ring during an inspection of the club floor earlier, an instinct that the welt of experience had left on her.

It stung her every day, when she was walking in the light of the ordinary. When it was not necessary to price up the men she met. When it was necessary to trust someone.

Lap dancing was not a job for everyone. Some women stay just an hour, a day, a week and leave. The other dancers do not make it easy either. Nobody wants fresh competition.

"What's wrecking your head?" a voice behind her asked.

It was the man from the bar, holding two drinks. She smiled and took a cigarette from the packet on the table, then began to twirl it between her fingers.

"You won't believe me," she said. "Maths."

He laughed.

"Why," he asked.

She tilted her head, examining him.

"I'm the accountant," she said.

He was sold.

****

His name was Dave. He was at the club with a recently separated friend, who he left sitting at the bar, once the barman told him Viola was drinking a Dazzler. She introduced herself, then pointed at the sofa. He sat down, listening with a fixed smile, as she revealed she was studying accountancy. That she had sat an exam last week. And waiting for the results was pure torture. A lot of dancers use fake stories.

Viola, however, could not lie.

When she did, she would forget what she said and make a fool of herself. But she did not tell the men everything either, just enough to get them to start sharing. Then, she sat back, smiled and listened.

Perching on the edge of the sofa, she angled herself toward the room, while leaning in to listen to Dave. Some of the men wanted nothing more than counselling. They did not buy dances. They might tip her. But it was not enough.

Not for what Viola needed.

She continually worked the floor with a flick of her hair, by shifting her thighs and playing with the cigarette in her hand. Those that spied on her from across the room, sat with reddening cheeks as her painted nails tap-tapped the table, teasing them.

She was in command.

"Let's go for a dance," Dave said.

Intriguing Viola, he stood up, demanding her full attention. She surveyed him curiously, then put the cigarette back in its box.

"Yes sir," she replied.

As seductively as she could, she led the way to the dance parlour, swaying her bouncing hips. When she ascended the staircase, the light from above shone down between her thighs. Dave tailed her quietly, eyeing her, with his hand gripping the rail.

At the top of the stairs, he paid for his dance before entering the parlour, where there were different sized cubby holes with two security men guarding them. Viola appreciated their presence. But it was awkward. She never liked a big audience.

She crossed the floor without looking at the security guards. She reached her dance room, pinched the black chiffon curtain, turned and held it open for Dave. He stepped through and she followed, pointing at the cushioned alcove, signaling him to sit down.

He did what he was told. She closed the curtain.

When she first started dancing, she could not keep time. She would go over by a minute and the other dancers would complain about her, as if she was trying to give the men a free stir.

The dancers would say anything to get rid of each other. But Viola would never give the men anything that they did not pay for. The very thought of it made her skin crawl.

Now that she had her routine, she did the same thing over and over, unless a customer kept buying minutes off her. Then, she would do more of what he liked.

Maybe pull her G-string down a bit.

That was it.

Grooving to the music, she was hypnotic. The sweat beneath her eyes brandished their blue, every time she lifted her head to look at her customer. It was as if a great passion had consumed her. She was, after all, a professional.

She was thinking about the bins at home, when he reached out to put a hand on her. She slid out of reach, before standing up.

"Times up," she said and walked out.

If he wanted more time with her, he would have put the money down. As he now had something to think about, he might want more later.

Back downstairs, Dave's newly separated friend was sitting at her table. She began to walk toward him, when the club door swung open and a group of drunken men stumbled through it, singing bawdy ballads. They wore GAA jerseys and dribbled with excitement.

Viola knew they would need a few moments to orientate themselves at the bar. Once they had acclimatised, they would spend their money. She introduced herself to Dave's friend, who ordered her another Dazzler and spoke too quietly for her to hear a word.

By the time Dave returned, two of the men in jerseys were sitting at a table opposite her, cracking jokes about their companions. They were celebrating a hurling match that they had won earlier in the day.

Dave and his friend excused themselves when they finished their drinks. Viola was disappointed, until she reckoned she would make more money. She was tired and the drunken men were amusing themselves.

It was not long before all three women were working them.

"This is a disgrace," the eldest man shouted.

He was looking directly at Viola, when he slammed his bottle of beer on the table. She looked away, shaking her head and laughing.

The judgemental types always looked at her like she should know better. But it was they who should know better. She was making more money in a night than they would in a week.

"Shut up will ya," a man retorted. "Ya old fart."

There was laughter.

Viola enjoyed the fellas sticking up for her. But she did not need them to. She had been taking care of herself for a long time and had been with her fair share of men.

She knew how to handle an idiot.

It was the middle-class types with their perfect lives, wives, careers and Range Rovers that annoyed her. They acted as if they were above her. And believed it too.

They came in looking for filth. They made her sick.

Once they were spending their money though, she smiled and took it, or as much as she could stomach. If they tried to touch her, she was happy to explain the rules.

One of the GAA players, Caleb, was Viola's type: tall, dark and funny.

She was chatting to him, with her limbs lightening and lifting as he spoke. She could have forgotten where they were, if he had not asked the question men always ask when there's a spark between them and a dancer.

"Why are you here?" he inquired.

She sat back and looked away from him, pushing herself back into the sofa. The question stripped her more than any piece of clothing she could have removed. But she did not squirm.

She straightened up, took out a cigarette and reset her glare.

"Why do you think?" she asked, looking at him.

"The money," she answered.

Breaking the smoke in half, she extinguished the spark. Then, it was back to business.

"Let's go," he said.

****

Upstairs in the dance parlour, Caleb paid for three dances. Viola turned away from him coyly, once she saw him take out his cash. Crossing the room without turning back, she looked like a snack as the light drizzled over her. She was smiling. She had just stacked up the night's profit in her head, when she reached the chiffon curtain, took a breath and erased every trace of her delight. It was not included in the price.

Some of the dancers wanted to be models or actresses. They hoped a rich man would walk in and save them. Viola did not need saving. She needed their money.

She wanted a house.

Her accounting job had paid for her final accountancy tuition. But it would not pay for somewhere to live. Not when she was the sole earner.

She looked back at Caleb, with one hand on her hip. She tugged on the curtain, then held it open for him. He stepped through with his eyes gorging on her.

She shifted from foot to foot.

"Sit," she demanded.

Closing the curtain behind her, she began to perform the extended version of her routine, while going over her grocery list in her head. She forgot why she had thought Caleb was handsome. Once he was a customer, he was nothing other than money to her.

It was the same with each and every one of the men, even the handful off the internet she had slept with. She did what she had to do while spending their money.

She never slept with anyone from the club. What she did in her free time was her business. The club's customers were off limits. If she broke the rules, she could not work for a week; she had not yet met a man who was worth that.

She never slept with a man for anything less than four hundred either. And she always had a friend who knew where she was, waiting for her to call.

It was not difficult to have sex for money. Some people cannot wash down the idea. But that meant nothing to her. They could not judge her. She had never set foot inside a lap dancing club before she applied to work in one. Before she really needed the money.

When she realised how much there was to be made, it was difficult to stay away. Once they are in the game, all the dancers change.

The fetish work was the easiest. The men usually smelt her feet, then were done and she was out the door. But not before checking she had every penny due.

She had to kiss a few of them too, which was repulsive, considering she had never kissed anyone she did not fancy. She had to repeatedly remind herself what the money was for.

The parlour lights flashed twice above her, signalling the club was closing, just as she was shaking the booth with her grand finale. She stepped down off the cushioned seat, fixed her hair and adjusted her underwear. Then, she took a playful bow.

"Until next time," she said.

Without hanging around to see the look left in his eyes, she hurried downstairs and smiled when she saw that the other dancers had given up on the men, who were finishing their drinks. Waving goodbye, she stepped out the staff door.

When she reached the dancers' dressing room, she was the last one in. The others were changing, taking turns to use the sink. They rarely felt the need to speak, except for the odd curse or hiss, when they remembered something the men had done or said.

She washed her face and put on a tracksuit. Her car keys and bag were ready to go. She never stayed for a drink or a chat. She wanted her cash and her bed.

Back at the bar, the boss was closing the tills. The money in the dance parlour cash box had already been counted. It was separated into shares on the counter.

"Bit of a head on you tonight, Vee," he said.

She blushed.

"Did the trick," she replied. "Didn't it?"

He handed her €470, which she folded and put in her bag. She never asked too many questions. Or answered many either. She said goodbye and walked out.

Her car was parked in the nearby 24-hour garage. Once she was sitting in it, she examined her face in the rear-view mirror. Without her makeup, the skin beneath her eyes was a dark purple, as if plump petals had been plucked from her fatigue.

It was 3.30 am.

She drove out of the city with the window down and a lit cigarette in her mouth. The wind cleansed her as she moved in silence. The sound of the city stripped itself from her ears.

She was exhausted and her back ached from the size of her breasts. Since the age of 12, they were the first thing any man noticed about her. She never had a great opinion of men because of it. But it was the club that slayed her dreams of romance.

She parked outside her little apartment: the downstairs half of her landlord's home. There were no lights on in the estate. She took a breath and held her bag tight.

Inside, she quietly locked the door to her one-bedroom apartment. Her mother was asleep on a fold-out bed, snoring in the middle of the living room. Viola smiled while tucking her in and headed straight for the bathroom.

After showering and getting ready for bed, she tip-toed over to her bedroom door, gently opened it and stepped inside. When she found the precious bundle buried beneath the blanket, she cast all her worries aside.

"Eve," she whispered.

Her daughter turned to her, reaching out her hands. Viola leaned down, kissed her warm cheek and hugged her tightly. Then, she sat up, placed that night's wage in a hole she had poked in their mattress, lay back down and fell asleep with Eve in her arms.

At 19, Viola became pregnant. She had just started her accountancy training, when Eve's father decided to leave the country. There was nothing Viola could say to make him stay, so she decided she would never let herself or Eve need him again.

She would take care of everything.

In the morning, the alarm woke them. They brushed their teeth and their hair, got dressed and had their breakfast together, with barely a foot between them.

Viola's mother was sitting on the sofa, drinking coffee and reading. She stayed over when Viola had to work. And avoided Eve's questions about her mother's job.

Viola's parents wished she had not told Eve about the club. But Viola would not lie to her daughter. Nor would she ever leave Eve alone with a man.

Kissing Eve goodbye, Viola waved as she watched her mother drive her to school. Viola usually had some study to do. But that morning, she had nowhere to be.

She put her feet up.

On the kitchen table in front of her was a bouquet of hand-picked violas, her favourite flower. There was a letter propped proudly amongst them. She picked it up and sniffed it long and hard. It smelt better than the cash upstairs.

It arrived yesterday, congratulating her on passing her final accountancy exam. She would be fully qualified by the end of the year, which meant a promotion, more money and most importantly, just a few more months working at the club. Then, she would have enough for their new beginning.

She fanned herself with the letter, addressed to Ms. Vivienne…

IV

THE SHOPKEEPER

9.00 AM WEDNESDAY, NOVEMBER 2ND

THE DOOR to Little Treats was wide open. Joy was standing in the middle of the shop floor, wondering why. It was happening to her a lot of the time. She would forget what she was doing. Or why she entered a room. At 72, it was testing her patience. She was scowling as she stared at the redbrick houses on the opposite side of the street, demanding an explanation to come to mind. When a sliver of light cracked through a slate of dark cloud, illuminating the windows and the car windscreens, it distracted her. Snatching her from the moment, it plunged her into the past.

Her silver brow softened with the comfort of remembering. Her sterling eyes smiled. She did not have to think twice about her life inside Little Treats.

Precisely 43 years ago, her husband, Roddy, chose the name when they bought the house and converted the living room into a shop. They did not know what they were getting themselves into, just that if they were together, they did not need anything else.

Rain or shine, they were behind the till, holding hands and hoping that everything worked out. They never neglected their duties. Or revealed the secrets confided in them.

They were an inseparable pair, who were the only shopkeepers on the street, under the shadow of Croke Park. They never got to attend a match because they could not afford to miss the business that it brought to their door; instead, they sat and shared a chocolate bar, while listening to the game on the radio, waiting for the stalls to empty.

When the streets filled with GAA supporters, Joy and Roddy were ready to greet them. Despite rarely having enough room or stock for all of them, the same happy faces returned, year after year, for a catch-up and a singsong.

Joy and Roddy never missed a day.

They knew they were particularly lucky. Especially when their four children came along. They got to spend all their time steadying their children's wobbles and catching their falls. Joy knew that not too many people got that chance.

Blessing herself, she snapped out of her trance.

"What are you doing?" she asked herself.

"This is ridiculous."

She unfolded her arms and shuffled towards the door, just as her neighbour, Caroline, stepped through it.

"Are you not freezing?" Caroline asked.

"Do you want me to close the door?"

Unsure of what she was supposed to be doing, Joy looked down at her feet, needing a moment to think; noticing that she was still wearing her pink furry slippers, she blushed, darkening the creases on her cheeks. She looked back up at Caroline, who was smiling.

"A bit of fresh air never harmed anyone," Joy said.

She spun around and sauntered back to the counter, knowing there was a reason the door was open. Promising herself she would figure it out afterwards, on her own, she turned on the kettle beneath the till, offered Caroline a brew and pointed at a stool.

Then, she adjusted her highchair, clambered up and leaned in to listen to Caroline speak about her family and her work. Struggling to keep up, Joy pinched at her white flannel shirt, thankful for the cold breeze that was blustering through the door, keeping her alert.

Each day, it was getting more and more difficult for Joy to remember the beginnings and the ends to the stories she heard or told. But what frustrated her the most was pretending, as whenever she tried to summon a thought, or act as if she grasped an entire idea, her mind tumbled away with the yarn it was spinning.

Lost in thought, she was frowning again.

"Joy," Caroline said. "Are you there?"

****

Joy was fixated on a shelf behind Caroline, where there were chocolate biscuits and beans beside tubs of brown sauce and a box of washing powder. Caroline waved a hand in front of her, scattering Joy's thoughts and sharpening the silence. Joy leaned back and looked up at her, with her hands and her pretences resting on the counter. She began to laugh wholeheartedly.

Caroline laughed with her.

"Oh dear," Joy said. "I feel very tired today."

Picking up her handbag, Caroline squeezed Joy's arm and said goodbye. She was just about to step outside when Joy called her name.

"Please love," Joy said. "Would you close the door?"

Caroline bent down and removed the doorstop, then left

the shop without saying another word. A moment later, a bell rang, shrill until it was quiet again.

Wild with panic, Joy jumped off her stool.

"Give me strength!" she said. "What was that?"

Shifting back, rocking on her feet, she inspected the door. The sunlight shredding through the wire-glass window lay like bars across her cheeks.

She set her rusty eyes on the top of the doorframe, where a gold bell glinted at her; the vague memory that she had of her son, hammering it to the wall, ruptured beneath its glare. Surely, she knew why it was there.

"There was never any need," she said, "before."

She was staring at the door, when it swung open and the bell rang; the morning got busier and the ringing got louder. Joy could not move from her seat for over an hour. By then, there was no change left in the till either. But she could deal with that after she dealt with the bell.

Walking over and opening the door with gritted dentures, she bent down and wedged the doorstop into place. Then, she rejoiced in the requiem of silence.

"There's nothing worse," she said, "than forgetting."

The wind blew over her, cooling her and her doubts. She checked the clock above the chocolate stand, shocked to see that it was past midday and the shop was in disarray. She began to tidy the nearest shelf.

Making her way around Little Treats, she moved with a blissful certainty and ease. She did not need to look at where her feet were going. Or what she had to do next.

The memories were set in her bones.

Lately, she had been worrying about what she would do without those four walls, enclosing her fondest memories.

When she was there, she simply had to look at the tears in the linoleum floor, the crooked shelves and the cracks, to remind her of her favourite stories.

"How am I supposed to close the door?" she asked.

"Everything I know is here."

She was born in Limerick, the eldest of 12 children. Her parents sent her to live with her aunt because there was no more room for her at home; she was ten years old.

The first train she ever saw took her all the way from the fields she used to play in, to the smouldering factory that was Dublin City, where there were women wearing furs, cars beeping and street vendors yelling. Joy had never seen anything like it.

It was a thrill. But it was not home. Not until she met Roddy.

By then, she was 19.

She had settled into the scene and gotten a job in a clothing store, despite the fact that she never wore anything fashionable, because she did not think it suited her. She was a small, stout woman, who preferred a well fitted shirt and a long, well ironed skirt.

The night she met Roddy, she was at a dance feeling awkward as usual, when a red-haired man started following her around the dancefloor. She shimmied away.

Roddy noticed her big eyes, her short dark curls and bountiful step, then her discomfort. He came over with his raucous hair and dashing smile, while Joy hopped with the delight of the butterflies tumbling in her tummy.

She had never been so unwilling to look away. Nor had she ever felt such a way.

"It's my turn," Roddy said.

Joy blushed.

She took his hand without hesitation. Roddy tucked his thick arm around her waist, pulled her closer and led the way. Every day after that, Joy followed Roddy, believing that she was truly lucky, because he was kinder than anyone she had ever met.

She was kinder because of him.

"I never knew," she said, "a person could do such a thing."

Standing behind the counter, Joy turned on the kettle. There was a picture of Roddy hanging on the wall beside her. She stretched over and stroked the polished glass that had separated them, since Roddy fell ill and died seven years ago; nothing had been the same.

It was only Little Treats that had not changed.

"Maam," a voice said.

"Maam!"

Joy gasped.

****

The American man standing at the counter was looking for the entrance to Croke Park. He could not apologise enough for surprising Joy, who could not understand why he had travelled all the way from the USA to see a giant GAA pitch. He must have thought she was half mad, pointing and stuttering, over and over, despite only having three directions to give. Feeling a chill, she looked at the open door.

The young man followed her gaze.

"Where are you from?" he asked.

She looked up at him.

"Limerick," she said. "It's a wonder how I never lost the accent."

Taking a bottle of water from the small fridge, the American stepped over to Joy, took out his wallet and handed her a €50 note. Joy keyed in the sale. The cash-drawer burst open.

Then, the sound of emptiness clattered around the room.

Joy sighed with exhaustion.

Yesterday, it was her granddaughter's 21st birthday. Joy was up late, celebrating with her family at the greyhound track, where her bet on an old dog paid out.

"I'll be back in a minute," she said.

Perking up, she walked around the counter, stepped into the hall and retrieved her winnings from her coat pocket. When she returned to the shop floor, she saw the little hand that had been trying to grab a chocolate bar from her stand, more days than not, whip in and around the doorframe. The silhouette of the young boy, who it belonged to, was stencilled in light against the window.

Sitting on his red tricycle, empty handed, he tore off like a shred of silk into the day.

"Every day," Joy said, "I miss him."

Looking up at the bell, she no longer needed to wonder what it was for. She wanted to catch the boy, to tell him that he did not need to steal. He just had to say hello.

It was what Roddy would have done.

He had a way of noticing people before they noticed him. He could sense strangers' stories, what they needed or where they were going, simply by laying the oak of his eyes on them.

Joy was different.

"Maam," the American said.

Joy blinked.

Hurrying over to the counter, she handed the man his change and watched him leave. Once she put the money in the till, she walked towards the door.

On the days that any one of her seven grandchildren came to visit, she would shut the shop and let them have whatever they wanted. Her children visited more often than she felt necessary, considering that she did not want to be a burden.

She wanted them to have the life that she had.

The pitter-patter of tiny paws behind her sent her into a flapping joy. The sunlight flooding the doorway warmed her for the first time that day. Her grey curls shone like pearls.

She turned around and saw her silver bearded Jack Russell waddling towards her. Bending down, she removed the doorstop, knowing that the memories she needed would still be there in the morning. She locked the door and followed Jack into the hall, without looking back.

The bell rang out.

V

THE ENTERTAINER

5.00 PM WEDNESDAY, NOVEMBER 2ND

THE PERFORMERS' dressing room at The Hidden Tiger was small, damp and cramped. There were three mismatched tables with mirrors and lamps draped in feather boas. They had every kind of gel, powder and spray laid out on them. There were wigs, dresses and heels strewn from every corner too; if someone did not know what they were doing in there, they could really hurt themselves. At least, that was what Simon hoped.

At 8pm, he was hosting the bingo. He was one of three resident drag queens there, where everyone knew him as Pearl. That night, he was working alone.

That was not the problem. He was.

It was his sixth and final night working. He was exhausted. His bloodshot eyes were a testament to the edge that he was about to tip over.

Silently, he undressed behind a ripped partition, wishing that the night had already ended. That he could go home.

Earlier that day, he had turned down a job as a makeup artist in London. With the residency and an increasing number of bookings across the city, he was making quite a celebrity out of Pearl. But for her to thrive, he had to put himself aside.

On that evening, he did not want to.

He stepped out, wearing a pink silk robe that parted as he walked to his makeup station, revealing his long skinny legs that did not seem to end. He sat down on a cushioned stool, adjusted the lamp and the mirror, then the strength of his vodka martini.

He did not see a reason to remain sober. Nobody cared, once Pearl was there.

Simon necked half the drink, refilled it and got to work. The first step to erasing what he could of himself, was to shave off everything from the waist up, which he took care of before arriving at work. He began to comb and gel back his thick auburn hair.

His freckles and high cheek bones were defined by the paleness of his skin. It kept him looking like the young Kerry boy he used to be.

He stopped and took another swig of his drink.

It was his fourth year working as a drag queen. He had never considered it as a career, or thought about the money, which was better than he could have imagined.

He grew up in a small town, where he never knew what he wanted to be because he never had a chance to be himself. By the age of five, all he knew was that he fancied boys, and that in a small town like his, it meant that the air turned to whispers wherever he went.

He was afraid of what people might say, even though he knew they were saying it anyway.

By nine, he had outgrown his Barbie dolls, alongside his trust in most people. He used to play with a boy two years older than him, who grew up down the road from him. One day, the boy kissed Simon, when he was not expecting it.

He and that boy kissed for over nine years. Simon never told a soul because the boy had told him not to. That boy is married now, with three children.

That was small town life. Simon shivered.

It was time for him to get rid of his eyebrows. He glued and flattened them down. Then, he covered himself in three shades and layers of foundation. By the end of the first hour, he had created a blank canvas.

Pearl was next.

****

Downstairs the bar had just opened. Simon turned on the radio to drown the noise. There were many fine lines between him and Pearl. So many small differences and shadows to be invented, that Simon had to hover over every detail. In the mirror, his face was as plain as a mannequin's. His brown eyes were the last trace of him. Running them over his painted skin, checking for blotches and finding none, he smiled and let the pride linger. He knew too well that he was only there because he was one of the best.

Selecting an assortment of brushes and gels, he laid them out and topped up his drink before beginning to draw on two new eyebrows. His hands moved surgically as he began to transform himself. No matter his mood, he had to perform.

There were plenty of wannabees willing to stab him in the back for his spot. He knew this because his hands were not clean. He had destroyed costumes, told some lies and withheld messages. He was not proud of it. But he was employed, which meant he had to keep up his act or those wannabees would be all over social media, dragging him down.

They would do anything for a crown.

When he turned 18, he came out to his parents, who said they always knew and loved him, then drove him to Dublin to study communications. Along the way, Simon realised he was leaving nothing behind. That was the first time he tasted freedom.

He moved into a house with four girls who adored him, who did his makeup and taught him how to walk in heels. He was no longer the talk of the town, just a boy who liked boys and did not mind putting on his friends' dresses, if it put a smile on their faces.

He no longer worried about what other people said about him. All those years of saying nothing had loaded his tongue with a response to every remark that he never pulled the trigger on. It came in handy when he made his first drag appearance.

His friends signed him up for a college talent show; got him drunk, dressed him up and pushed him on stage, where everything fell off him. He vowed never to do it again.

By then, he was skipping most of his classes to help his roommate, who was training to become a makeup artist. Simon was fascinated by everything that she worked on; he would stand at her shoulder until she let him help.

Believing that he could do better, he dropped out of college and signed up for a yearlong course in makeup artistry, promising himself he would be the best. He never missed a class. Or a high grade. The following year, he taught the course.

Another hour later, Pearl was looking like herself, while Simon's drink was untouched. He took a big gulp, stood up and turned up the radio, stifling the noise from downstairs.

When he was ready, he walked back behind the partition, where he spent most of the next hour dressing. He was bent over with his fingers pinning a purple wig to his head, when there was a knock on the door.

"Yo!" the DJ yelled. "Pearl!"

Simon rolled his eyes.

"Ten minutes to showtime," the DJ shouted.

Peering through his legs at the closed door, Simon shook his head to ensure that the wig was secure. Once he was satisfied, he stood up and threw the long ringlets back off his face, which was utterly changed. Up close, there were slight hints of the tricks that he might have played. But who cared? Simon was no longer there.

He was now Pearl.

Wearing red fishnet tights and a red and yellow tartan skirt and blazer, Pearl, in a pair of red platform boots, was eight inches taller than Simon. The black leather gloves and choker were Pearl's signature; another line drawn between Simon and Pearl.

Some people believed he wanted to be a woman. That he must be missing something in life because he dressed up as one for work. He no longer had the time to change their minds.

The only problem Simon had with his career was finding the opportunity to display his skills; as he did not want to be a woman, he could not use them on himself. He began to create different personas, photograph them and post them on social media.

An events manager saw them online, contacted him and offered him a place in a drag competition. With money to be won, Simon could not refuse.

He came third and brought home some vouchers, alongside a thirst for first. Once he started winning, his drag career took off. He had not allowed himself to stop earning. To think about anything other than his spot at the top. Or what he had to do to stay there.

After a heavy misting of hairspray, he turned off the radio. The boom of the crowd beneath his feet hauled him out of his head. He polished off his drink and took one final look at Pearl in the mirror; it was the last time that all of his work would be in the right place.

"Ready?" he asked himself.

He laughed.

Capturing the corners of the smile he had just conjured, he shimmied out of the room, down the corridor and the stairs to the backstage area. There was a stage assistant standing by the red velvet curtain, peeping out at the empty stage. When he saw Simon, he began to wave.

Simon hurried over, until the heat pulsing off the crowd hit him. Then, he stopped, closed his eyes and inhaled the energy.

"Are you ok?" the stage assistant asked.

Simon looked up from under a thick set of false lashes, grinning. He lifted his head, tossed the purple ringlets off his shoulder, strode over to the curtain and pinched it.

Disappearing into silence, he altered his angles and softened his silhouette.

"Showtime," he whispered.

Letting go of the curtain, he shifted from side to side, balancing on the wings of the butterflies in his stomach. He took a deep breath and a firm grip on his nerves, stuck his hand past the velvet and twirled a leather covered finger in the spotlight.

When he withdrew it, slowly, the stage assistant tapped his microphone.

"Good evening, everyone," he announced.

The crowd hushed and howled.

"Please welcome your host, Pearl."

The DJ played a drum roll, while Simon counted to three before stepping out, past the curtain, where he let Pearl take control.

****

Sashaying across to the microphone, Pearl's curls bounced inches below the ceiling. She ignored the crowd that was straining to look up at her. There was a table with a drink waiting for her on it. All she wanted was a sip as the spotlight followed her, bringing the shimmer of Simon's disguise to life. She reached the table, picked up the glass and finished the drink. When she leaned into the microphone, the crowd leaned with her.

"I'll take another one," she said.

The crowd erupted.

She knew exactly what they wanted from her. How to cross the lines that they would not. How to comfort their madness by revealing her own. That way, they did not have to be afraid to be themselves. In fact, Pearl dared them to embrace themselves, by reminding them that they were all outsiders. That she too, did not belong. Except on that stage.

"Hello bitches," she mouthed.

Shaking her chest and plumping her purple hair, she stared down at the audience. With their bingo slips, their pens and their hungry hearts, they were ready to eat her up. She began to compliment them, and condescend to them, while winking at some of the men.

Then, she explained the rules.

They were playing musical bingo, which meant that the DJ would play snippets of different songs, until one lucky player marked off a full row on their slip. The more winning slips, the more free drinks, which meant that it was a long two hours.

Dancing, lip-syncing and death-dropping to the music, the sweat dripping off Pearl was just as dramatic as her performance. When it was time to give away the last of the free alcohol, her voice was raw from roaring and her wig was clinging on.

Her mascara had begun to run too. But who cared?

No matter how many of her lines were blurred, the crowd still looked up to her, swinging from the rafters.

"Goodnight bitches," she said.

She bowed.

The audience cheered for more. But Simon was done.

****

Behind the curtain, the crackle of the crowd's electricity spiked the air that Simon was breathing. He was buzzing. With just an hour to be spent mingling with the audience, his shift was nearly over. He whipped off his small tartan coat, made his way up the stairs and down the corridor, wearing the confidence Pearl had gifted him, like it was a diamond necklace. Without her, he knew he would be different. That his life would be easier.

Reaching the dressing room door, he heard Precilla and Fab Fanny chatting inside. He swung his coat over his shoulder, threw open the door, strode towards them and twirled before sitting down at his makeup station.

Precilla and Fab Fanny clapped.

They were in their robes, finishing off their makeup, with their wigs brushed and hung up beside them. Simon fixed himself a drink, while catching up with their conversation, laughing and filling them in on his show; they did not need to know about the job in London.

They were his friends. That was his business.

After retouching his makeup, he showered his wig with more hairspray, stood up, wished the queens luck, picked up his drink and left. Walking down the main staircase, he lifted his chin and his shoulders as he slipped back into Pearl's persona.

The crowd touched and grabbed him, passing him around; they took pictures and asked him questions about his private life. Or rather, Pearl's.

Simon answered what he could, until the heat and the pressure of what people believed became too much. Excusing himself to get a drink, he pushed through the heaving bodies that stood between him and the exit. He did not hear his name being called, over and over.

"Simon! Simon!"

He pushed on.

Outside, the fresh air hit him like a clean sheet; if fewer people had been about, he would have dropped to his knees to inhale it. Instead, he bummed a smoke off a stranger.

A moment later, a hand touched his shoulder.

"Simon!" a woman said.

He tilted his head.

"Simon!"

Jolting with surprise, Simon turned around to see his old roommate, Suzanna, who was laughing with exasperation.

"Well?" she asked. "What happened?"

Simon stared at her, confused. He could not understand her concern. Then, he remembered that he had told her about the job offer in London. Explaining to her the reason why he did not accept it, she let out a breath and held his hand.

"You're doing too well," she said, "to stop now."

Simon hugged her.

Honestly, he never expected someone to be looking for him there. He did not hang out there because people usually asked for Pearl.

With hands poking and pulling at him, he excused himself and got back to the show. The next moment he had to himself, he checked the time and ran up the stairs, without saying another word. With the next show about to start, he was officially off the clock.

Inside the dressing room, he removed his wig and as much of his makeup as he could, before changing his clothes, packing his bag, walking out and down the stairs to the back door. Outside on the street, in a pair of jeans and green parka-coat, he flagged a taxi, hopped in and took out his two phones, checked them and put them away.

He had come to realise he needed a separate phone for business, when his own life could not keep up with Pearl's social media. Some people did not know where to draw the line.

On an average day, Simon received two or three messages from questionably straight men, asking what Pearl was wearing and offering to buy her things, as if Simon was sitting at home, wearing a wig and heels. Honestly, he did not understand it.

He liked to hike and go for coffee, to sit at home in his bathrobe and slippers, watching TV. He wanted to find love too. But anytime he got close, Pearl got in the way.

He had to give his drag career an expiration date. He would not spend his life defining or defending the line between him and Pearl.

At 28, he would hang up his wig. Until then, he would not rest.

He rolled down the window, just as the taxi crossed the River Liffey, heading north of the city that was already singing beneath the street lights. The wind tickling his skin with the cold, reminded him of being buried neck deep in the sand along the coast of the small town where he grew up; when he was just eight years old and his mother was calling his name, over and over, against the breeze off the ocean.

He had ignored her.

"Little Pearl," she called.

He looked at her, like it was the first time he had ever been seen.

Interlude Pt. III

M.A.D.

11.40 PM WENESDAY, NOVEMBER 2ND

Peddling down O'Connell Street, I could barely breathe with the speed I was going. I did not think about slowing. I was choking the words in my throat, refusing to speak them or believe them. I pushed harder and wrestled the wind, grunting as it licked the surrender off my skin. I cycled across the paths and headed for the Royal Canal. My arms and legs were aching. My bare knuckles and cheeks were stinging, though the feeling was better than the pain twisting its blade in my ribcage. How had I made it so far, just to crumble and cave?

I knew something was going to break. Unfortunately, it looked like it was me.

The words of a hotel guest, who was dressed in shabby faux fur and pearls bigger than her, had been throbbing against my temples since I finished my shift earlier that night. I had been trying to carve them out; but I could not mute my mind or stop rewinding my costly smile.

"How much do you make?" she had asked, while teetering on her tippy toes.

"Surely, it can't be much?"

Her husband had walked away, bowing his head. The woman did not flinch. Or shoot a glance his way. Instead, she stared down at me, with her mouse sized eyes.

"Not enough," I replied.

The woman feigned a smile, fracturing the lines on her face, along with the lies in her sincerity. Handing over her room key, I grinned sweetly, then wished her a pleasant stay.

I was not paid to teach kindness.

Arriving at the bridge over the canal, I cycled to the top, hopped off my bike and propped it against the bulging stone. The wind nudged me forward, murmuring wistfully in my ear.

I leaned on the bridge and peered down at the canal resting below, resembling a black satin scarf that was dressing the streets with its promise of tranquillity and sheer nothingness. I always wondered how many souls had stood and stared down at it, pouring themselves into it, hoping it would carry them away. And how many others were swept away because the only people that could help were drowning in the same formidable waters.

I could not look any longer.

Grabbing my bike, I pushed it down the bridge. I stormed my way past the derelict houses, the freshly painted homes, the trees marked by tragedy and the graffiti screaming from the walls and the railway track, claiming the city back. I thought of the people, who had given me their time and their trust, just so I could write this book.

In that moment, the darker parts of me struck, heckling me and reminding me that no matter how much I tried, I did not have enough time to tell their stories and continue mine. I was inching down a tightrope, without an inkling of the thin line stretched out before me.

Crossing the Tolka River, my head was heavy and hanging low, when a glass bottle smashed on the concrete a few feet in front of me. I did not skip a heartbeat.

I stopped and slowly looked across the street, where the young boy I had fallen over , was standing beside his tricycle, with the flats watching his back. He stared at me, pitilessly as the barrel of a gun, blowing me out of my emotional eclipse.

Then, he smiled, revealing the child he was.

I straightened myself up, while he spun his tricycle around. Plonking himself on the saddle, he peddled through the gateway of the flats, tick-tick-ticking out of sight, into the lungs of the night. I stood still and laughed, knowing he was not trying to hurt me.

He was letting me know that he was there.

That he saw me.

VI

THE FIGHTER

0.00 PM THURSDAY, NOVEMBER 3RD

On the edge of his bed, Tommy sat rocking himself back and forth. Shifting his weight from one foot to the other, his trailer-home creaked beneath him. His hands were in fists, held tight against his chest, rubbing knuckle to knuckle. For the third night in a row, the open-eyed nightmares had him staring into the dirty grey wallpaper, thinking about his father, about dying young and all the things that Tommy had done wrong.

It could not go on. Or else, he would not.

Heaving himself off the bed, he fumbled out of his bedroom, cursing and grunting at the dark. He had been too lazy to fix the light. Or to ever adjust to the size of his trailer. The five stones he had put on over the last year, was not helping him either.

He pushed himself through the narrow doorway, stumbled into the kitchen and switched on the light. The wind was whistling outside, carrying the chirps of a lost bird from the trees; reaching up, he shut the window tight.

Taking a pizza from the compact freezer in the corner, he removed it from its packaging, put it in the oven and set the heat. His stomach grumbled, sickening him.

The bin was overflowing.

Holding the empty pizza box, looking for somewhere to put it, he realised every surface was covered in junk and takeaway cartons, clothes that no longer fitted him and books he had not read. The rage spewed out of him instantly.

He could not control it. Nor did he have to.

Kicking open the trailer door, he started to throw the rubbish outside. His anger rose with each layer of filth he unearthed. His family peeped out from their neighbouring windows, holding their breaths.

They knew better than to chance lifting the lace curtains. If he was not in the mood to see or talk to anyone, they knew to stay away.

He banged down the steps, into the darkness, where he stormed around, gathering pieces of wood and throwing them on the mound of rubbish that lay between his trailer and his brother's. Then, he poured some petrol over them, lit a match and flicked it.

When the fire burst into existence, he took a step back.

Staring at the flames, he took his t-shirt off, wiped his forehead with it and threw it on top. Pulling out a cigarette from his tracksuit bottoms, he sparked it and inhaled its smoke.

With the blazing trash chasing the shadows off his skin, the tattoo of his name across his back glistened as his sweat rolled down it. He told himself that now was not the time to worry about the windows of the hotels and businesses around him, bearing down on him like bloodless eyes. The people inside those buildings could think whatever they wanted.

He was a traveller. He had no say. He coughed and spat on the fire.

Behind him, the coldness of the clear night had shushed and shut the doors of Dublin's largest social housing estate. Some people called it The Jungle.

Tommy was eight years old, walking through the estate on the way home from school, when a lad ran up and punched him in the face. It was nothing unusual, except that day when he got home, nursing a black eye, his mother told him his father had taken his own life with a shotgun. That was when Tommy went numb.

He would have done anything for his father, who suffered from schizophrenia. At the time, his mental illness was worsening, which meant he needed more help than he was willing to ask for, never mind take. Still, Tommy never understood why his father did it.

Not until now.

With nothing but regrets and €400 of his drug money left, a shiver of shame turned his head away from the flames. He stared at his trailer.

Noticing the windows were clouded, he sprinted up the steps and spotted smoke billowing from the oven; rushing over and opening it, he took a step back. When the scorched air passed, he saw the burnt pizza, slammed the oven door, turned around and put both of his fists through the wall.

By then, there were no more birds to frighten in the trees.

****

Shaking and sitting, standing and walking from the sofa to the kitchen, Tommy gazed down at his knuckles. The fire writhing wildly outside, no longer held his interest. He was somewhere else, rattling behind the bars of his silence. Lighting another cigarette, he smoked it furiously. The ignited memory of his father was spreading within him, scorching the edges of his sanity. He had to keep moving. Or he might go alight with it.

At first, he did not believe it. Not his father. Not the fighter. He could not have left him.

Not his boy Tommy.

It was not until the day of the funeral and the closed coffin that Tommy finally understood why his father was not coming home. That he was dead.

Tommy spent the whole ceremony trying to wrap his head around it. He stared at the coffin, hoping it was a sick joke. Afterwards, his uncle put an arm around his shoulder, took him aside and shielded him from the rest of his family.

"You are the man now, Tommy," his uncle said.

Tommy cried.

It was the last time he showed any kind of weakness. If he wanted to be the man his family needed, he had to keep his grief to himself. He could not speak of his father either, as just hearing his mother call the name Tommy shared with him, was agonising.

His family did not have to ask how he was because he was coming home with broken noses and busted lips. He had to fight the kids from The Jungle and from school, who were always making fun of him for being a traveller. Then, he had to fight the kids from the other halting sites, who made fun of him for not having a father.

They called him a sissy. He could not walk away.

His father had taught him how to fight. He would watch Bruce Lee, Van Damme and Seagal films, then teach Tommy and his two younger brothers the martial arts moves. He would laugh at them when they took it too seriously. And they would laugh back at him, before tackling him. There was nothing better than seeing him smile.

He was their hero. Their very own Mike Tyson.

He did whatever he could for them and their mother. She used to sit and watch as they re-enacted the historic fight scenes, with the long grass of the green beside the halting site scratching at their knees. There were two raggedy horses that roamed there freely, oblivious to the beeping traffic and the hard beady eyes that lined the windows of the passing cars.

Tommy did not notice them then either. He was happy.

Taking a step back from his memories, he had to remind himself to breathe. His heart was breaking as it beat against his chest. What if he dropped dead?

What would his mother do?

He sat down and started pounding his legs with his fists. Shaking his head, trying to rid himself of the dread coursing through him, he decided that if there was no way out, there had to be a way through. He roared like a lonely beast.

"Tommy! Tommy Boy!" his brother yelled. "What's goin' on?"

Tommy gripped his knees and gritted his teeth. His face was burning.

"G'way!" Tommy said. "G'WAY!"

His brother stood defiantly in the doorway, with the fire hissing behind him. He stared point blank at Tommy, who only tore his eyes away from his knuckles for a moment.

"Just tell me what you're feelin'," his brother said. "I won't make a fool of ya, I promise."

Tommy flinched, as if he took a blow to his stomach. He covered his face. The snort that shook his body a second later, broke the stitching of the words that had sewed his mouth shut. He dropped his hands and looked at his brother with tears in his eyes.

"I feel shite!" he said. "And I'm fat!"

They laughed.

Then, they sunk into silence. They had never talked about their feelings. But there was no more time for either of them to play the hardman. Tommy was deadly serious.

He had no options. No prospects.

His girlfriend had left him six months before. He was lonely and broke. He had to stop selling drugs because everyone was dying. He could not box either, he had no hunger for it.

Maybe the whispers were true. Maybe he was a good-for-nothing pikey. Without another word said, he dropped his head and ran his fingers over the back of his neck.

His brother backed out the door, ran past the fire and into his trailer. His pregnant girlfriend was sleeping. He did not want to wake her. Tommy had scared her earlier, when she saw him throw his boxing gloves, and everything else, out the door.

Tommy's brother had snuck out to salvage the gloves, while Tommy was looking for more firewood. After finding them, he returned to Tommy.

"Here," his brother said. "You need to do something positive."

With the gloves dangling in front of him, Tommy looked up. The gloves were worn soft and their threads were pulled and stained. They looked older than he remembered. But then, he had not looked at them since he lost his last fight three years ago.

His face twitched and tightened.

"That's enough," Tommy said. "Go back to bed."

As he stood up, he snatched the gloves from his brother. He wanted to feel the blue leather, imprinted with the man he had fought so hard to be.

When he felt nothing, he threw the gloves on the sofa.

Outside, he looked down at the dying fire, snarled and walked off into the darkness, gathering wood and wondering if the gloves would even fit him now.

Or if he would trust himself in the ring again.

****

Boxing was all about movement. It was setting traps and jabbing, planning how to give punishment without receiving any. Fighting was different. It was aggression. It was getting inside your opponent's head and overloading them with punches. Instinctually, Tommy was a fighter. He wanted to go toe-to-toe. To dance the bloody mamba. He would snap a rib or shatter a jaw, just to prove he was a man. To him, there was no better way.

At 12, he was tired of being beaten up and seeing his mother worrying. He joined the boxing club beside the halting site, bought his first pair of boxing gloves and made a list of those who had bullied him. Using his fury as fuel, he trained five times a week.

Every morning and evening, he would repeat the same moves until his muscles remembered every double left hander and duck. Better than he did.

Inside the ring, it was set, ready, touch gloves and box; nothing existed outside the ropes, except the trainers' voices, yelling instructions. He was never fully engaged and thinking.

He was reacting and adjusting to his opponent's style, while continually reminding himself that he had to move, keep his chin down, arm up and jab straight. That way, he was protected.

The aim was to prevent his opponent from landing points, although Tommy never had much patience for scorekeeping. Whoever did not get up, lost in his eyes.

He never looked worried, which unnerved the other fellas, who believed him when he told them he was fine. It was a lie, right up until he threw his first punch. Then, he was an unstoppable force. In the first six months, he made it to the All Ireland Boxing Final and won. He ticked off every name on his list too.

A year later, he took a stretch in height and went up a weight division. The fellas he fought were still going down, just not as quick as Tommy was used to, which made it more interesting, more satisfying for him when his anger triggered and he put them away.

He was the champ.

Back inside his trailer, he put his left leg in front of his right, then began to spar at the air. Ducking and dodging, he controlled his breathing for the first time that night: he did not sound like he was dying. But then, it was never his form or style that let him down.

It was his head.

At 15, he left school because his cousins were making a fool of him for going. He got an apprenticeship in carpentry, while training every day. He had not lost a fight, or missed a day's work, and still, he could not sleep. He could not lie in bed, staring at the ceiling, worrying about being the big man either. Not when people were afraid of him.

He would often find himself lurking around the edges of The Jungle, smoking and sniffing out trouble. His cousin, Paul, a settled traveller, lived there.

Two years older than Tommy, Paul had made a fortune selling coke and heroin. He was operating at such a high level that he needed someone he could trust to protect him.

Everyone knew Tommy.

If they did not, they had heard a story or two about the young traveller boy who went around knocking everyone out. Paul tried to recruit him for that very reason.

Tommy declined.

But eventually, he needed the distraction. He called his cousin, accepted his offer and went to work. The gear was ordered a month in advance from Africa. It would come in ounce bullets that had been wrapped in condoms and swallowed.

When it arrived, it was cut up and stored in different locations in Dublin. The heroin was weighed and bagged immediately. The coke was mixed with various substances for a bigger profit, which meant it had to be stashed for longer, adding to the cost and the risk. Once it was bagged, it simply needed to be delivered.

It was already sold before they placed the order with their boys in Africa. And as soon as they collected their money, they made another phone call.

It did not always go according to plan, which was where Tommy came in. Earning a couple of grand a week, banging down doors and busting heads, he was dousing his rage in blood and drugs, then falling into bed and sleeping soundly.

He was not thinking too much then either.

Boxing with bruised hands and ribs, he was still winning every time he stepped in the ring. He was just not sure why, as every time the referee held his arm up, all he could think of was what he had lost.

A year later, he had a match with an opponent he had previously beaten. He stayed out the night before partying, knowing he would not be fit to fight the next day.

His trainer noticed that something was not right. But Tommy chose to fight anyway. He was an animal. Afraid of nothing, except himself.

He was 10 points ahead and exhausted. In the third round, he started whispering to his opponent, trying to get inside his head and awaken whatever anger it held.

Tommy wanted to be hit. He wanted to be knocked out.

"Come on!" Tommy yelled.

His opponent answered by throwing punches he had never thrown before. Tommy was relieved, as each time he let his opponent hit him, the pain validated his own muted attack.

When his opponent won, Tommy pretended to be stunned. Then, he stormed out of the stadium, leaving his boxing gear behind.

Later that night, his trainer tried to return it. And persuade him not to quit. Tommy slammed the door on him.

The gear was still on the ground by his trailer the next morning. Tommy threw it in a corner and forgot about it. He was not that man anymore.

He told his cousin he wanted to take a step back from the beatings, which was not a problem: Tommy could hire his own men to do the dirty work. He could keep his hands clean, if he could keep them out of the messy business they were in.

With each passing year, new brands of competition came along. There were deathly disputes, surprise shooters and grievances that had to be squared. For every lost comrade or seized shipment, there was more money to be made and voids to be filled with the coke that they sniffed off the corner of their own coins. The clock was ticking on whoever was next.

It took two cousins overdosing on heroin, three murdered, three more in jail and hysterics from his mother, who thought that he was only selling hash, to make him question what he was doing. He even had an aunt dying from AIDS in hospital, while her son worked protection for him.

"Fuck!" he said.

"FUCK!"

Covering his ears with his hands, Tommy paced up and down his trailer. The last time he had tried to explain that the drugs were not cutting it, that he was not sleeping, his cousin was not listening. They were sitting in traffic on the way to one of his factories, when he hushed Tommy and told him to look in the car's rear-view mirror.

There were two guys, wearing only black, on a motorbike. They were racing up the middle lane of the motorway, smashing the mirrors of the other cars. Tommy panicked and tried to get out. But his cousin stopped him.

"They'll shoot," he said.

Ramming the car in front of them, he shot out of the lane and pulled into a halting site nearby, where he abandoned the car. Tommy hopped out and followed him.

After running a few miles through the fields, they took cover in a patch of tall grass and stayed hidden until it was dark. That was it for Tommy.

He was out.

Three months later, his cousin was arrested. Then, he was stabbed 11 times in prison. Tommy sat down on the couch, laid his head back and shut his eyes. The fire died outside. The birds returned to the trees.

If he was not that man anymore, who was he?

He fell asleep.

****

Waking up to the sound of his own snoring, Tommy sat upright and looked out at the morning, glazing the halting site. With a stiff neck and a bad taste in his mouth, he stood up and grabbed the clothes he had left, walked out and down the steps, onto the dirt and into the dawn. He snuck into his mother's trailer to shower, dressed and left the halting site. He did not look up. He did not want anyone, or anything, getting in his head.

He had made a decision.

With his brother's words ringing in his ears, like the bell before the next round, he decided he was going to finish school. He had been smart once. Maybe he could be again.

Cutting through The Jungle, he walked along streets that were still with slumber. It was his memories of the years spent fighting, throwing stones and watching people shoot up, pass out and get put out, that were awakening.

He stepped lightly, for his own sake.

It was going to take more than a day to fix him. He needed time. But he swore to himself that he would talk. As soon as he got home, he would sit down with his family and explain to them, in as few words as possible, how he had been feeling.

Reaching the social welfare office, he stood outside for 45 minutes, smoking cigarettes. When the door opened, he jumped from his trance and walked up to the desk, where he was told to take a number.

His phone rang. He silenced it.

After taking a ticket, he waited to be called, while silencing two more phone calls. Finally, his number binged up on the board above the service desk. He shuffled over and told the social welfare official what he wanted to do. Pulling at his sleeve and avoiding her stare, he looked younger than his age, quite like a boy he never got to be.

She assigned him an appointment with an employment assistant the following week, then gave him a leaflet detailing the different ways he could complete his Leaving Certificate. Smiling, she said goodbye.

Tommy blushed.

Outside, the sun was high. The wind was churning the cold. The people passing seemed to be in a hurry. He was enjoying the fresh air, feeling like he had put on a new pair of boxing gloves. Like he had finally done something good.

His phone rang again.

It was his mother, crying so much that he could barely understand her. Forcing himself to breathe, he curled his free hand into his fist.

"Slow down woman!" he said.

"What happened?"

The Gardai had arrived not long after Tommy left that morning. They threw his family out of their trailers, along with all of their belongings, then battered them because they felt they were not being co-operative. Wearing all black and helmets, guns and batons at the ready, their badges and names were out of sight.

"The bastards!" he said.

He hung up.

Running, sweating and panting, he barely made it to the

entrance of The Jungle, where he had to stop because his legs were wobbling beneath the weight of him. He put his hands on his knees and his head down, breathing long and hard, just as two young lads cycled by, laughing at him. He stood up, gave them the finger, started to run and spit again.

He needed two more spit stops before reaching the halting site. The gardai were nowhere to be seen. Nor was their warrant to raid the halting site down the road.

The destruction they caused was purpling on his family's arms and legs, and being swept and collected up off the dirt. Despite all of this, the Gardai did not return.

Or apologise.

It was nothing new to Tommy or his family. They had all been victims of discrimination at some point in their lives. Usually, it was a daily occurrence.

Tommy cursed himself for not getting there faster. For not helping them.

What kind of man did that make him?

He took the cigarettes from his pocket, threw them in the empty bin beside his mother's trailer, walked into his own, took off his jacket and dropped it on the sofa, with the Leaving Certificate leaflet in the front pocket. Picking up his old boxing gloves, he jogged back outside, called his brothers and told them to get their gear.

They were going training.

Walking down to the bottom of the halting site, where there was an old stone shed with two punch bags hanging inside, Tommy stepped in and warmed up. When he threw his first punch, dirt fell from the rafters, landing in his eyes.

He kept punching and blinking, knowing this time, he was fighting for his life.

Back in his trailer, his mother was looking for dirty clothes she could put in the wash. Finding the only jacket he had left, she picked it up and folded it over, letting the leaflet fall from Tommy's pocket. She took a look at it and returned it, before hanging up the jacket and swearing she would not mention it.

Not until he did.

That evening, when they sat around her table for dinner, her smile gave her away. But who could blame her?

She was the proud mother of a fighting man.

VII

THE MOTHER

10.00 AM THURSDAY, NOVEMBER 3RD

SHAUNA KNEW this was coming. She would be lying if she said otherwise. It was the thing about being a mother, she always imagined the worst. But then, never in her life did she think she would be standing on a bus, holding the handles of a buggy and hiding what she assumed was an ecstasy pill in her coat pocket. Maybe that was why it hurt so much. She should have known. Or at least noticed. Like any good mother would have.

She was changing her daughter's bed linen earlier, when a small bag of blue pills flew across the room. Shauna picked them up, assuming they were sweets, until she brought them downstairs, made a cup of tea, poured them on the kitchen table and counted all twenty, shaped like little ghosts. The smell of them burnt her nose.

She picked up the phone and called her mother, without sputtering a word or a tear. She blamed herself, then told herself she did not deserve to feel betrayed.

Her mother told her to call her uncle, Willy. He was a drug addict a decade ago; if he did not know what he was looking at, he would surely know someone who would. He spent a lot of his time at a homeless centre, checking in on his friends. He asked Shauna to meet him there in an hour.

Her daughter, Sara, was 15 years old.

"Jaysus," Shauna gasped.

Looking around at the other passengers on the bus, she shrank; though none of them were looking at her, she still imagined their pity filled stares. She avoided eye contact, fearing they would figure out her crime. Or tell her what she was already thinking.

She should have been at home folding the washing, putting the shopping away or cleaning. Anything other than standing on that crowded bus, headed toward the city.

Trying to disguise the dread gnawing at her nerves, she squeezed herself down to a crouch and checked her four-year-old daughter, Melissa, who was asleep in her buggy. Her blonde curls, strewn across her rosy cheeks, looked as if they belonged to an angel.

Shauna petted the plastic rain cover that separated them. Then, she settled her eyes on her own reflection, stood back up and wiped her face with her sleeve. With her long brown hair, tied into a low ponytail, she looked older than 33.

Her face and neck were covered in red patches, which happened whenever she was nervous. She looked guilty.

She had never robbed a thing. Or touched a drug before.

On the steps of the flats where she grew up, drugs were bought, shot and sold. The death, and everything else that came with them, was a horrible thing to swallow as a child.

Enough for Shauna to never try them.

She was the youngest of five children. The quietest too. She kept to herself, played with her baby doll, helped her mother and studied. She secretly listened to the chatter that clattered outside, but never stepped out from behind the door.

When she was 17, her parents got a house. It was a ten-minute walk from the flats: the fresh start they had been waiting for.

Shauna and her two older brothers moved in with her parents, which was convenient because her brothers were rarely at home. And because Shauna was pregnant.

There was no debate about giving up the baby. Nor could she have afforded to go to England. It was just that Shauna always knew she would be a mother.

Her boyfriend of five years, Paul, was the father. He was the same age as her, and from a flat nearby, where he secretly signalled meetings to sneak kisses from her. He was the love of her life, until she had Sara.

"Ma!" Melissa yelled.

The bus was parked on O'Connell Street. Everyone else was getting off.

"Alri' baby," Shauna said.

****

Out on the street, Shauna checked that the pill, wrapped in tissue, was still securely stuffed in the corner of her coat pocket. She sighed with relief once she was satisfied. She bent down and took another look at Melissa, who was sipping on her bottle. Standing back up, she zipped up her coat and took off. With the fresh air blowing against her skin, came the sting of the open wound. She kept her head down. She did not feel the need to look at the lifestyle she could not afford, heckling her from every door.

"Give us a break," she begged.

"Please."

The dark clouds bruising the sky were thickening, threatening rain. She quickened her pace. But there was no escaping it. When it came pouring down a minute later, she took shelter under a tree, while Melissa laughed in her buggy.

Shauna smiled at her.

Drops of rain ran down her nose, splattering against the plastic rain cover. Melissa kept trying to wipe them away. She was too young to know that she was salvaging the day.

When the rain stopped, Shauna carried on.

She never had big hopes, or dreams, just an idea of how her life would go. How she would be working when she got pregnant, studying or saving to buy a house or a holiday.

When she became a mother, she became nothing other.

Everything was about Sara.

Shauna and Paul were sharing a room in her parents' house, where Sara was sleeping in the bed between them, waking every few hours, crying. It took a long time for Shauna to figure out why. So sometimes, she cried too. But she never let Sara out of her sight.

She minded Sara when Paul went to work. She played with her, fed her, tickled her and read to her. She never missed a move Sara made.

"Righ'," she said, lifting her head

The homeless centre was up ahead. She crossed the road and parked the buggy behind a car, where all that Melissa could see was the pavement lined with slanting houses.

After handing her half a sandwich, Shauna took out her phone and called her uncle, who told her he would be out in a minute. Shifting from foot to foot, she put the phone away, then slid her hand into her coat pocket, checking that the pill was safe.

Finally, she stood still.

"Look at you," her uncle yelled.

She jumped.

Her hand shot out of her pocket, morphing into a wave before she dropped it. She tried lifting her lips into a grin. But that faded fast. She was in no mood for talking.

Her uncle looked happier and healthier than she had ever seen him, though the tightness of his skin over his bones never allowed the tell-tale signs of his old habit to leave him. Once he reached them, he embraced Shauna, then leaned down to greet Melissa.

Shauna took the piece of tissue from her pocket, flashed the pill at her uncle, then put it away. He stood up and asked if he could see it again.

"That's a yoke," he said. "Sorry! Ecstasy!"

Smiling like he had just won on the horses, her uncle gazed at her. She took a minute to herself, shaking and stuttering, while he looked in every other direction.

With the pill back inside her coat pocket, Shauna thanked her uncle and said goodbye. He did not look surprised, rather relieved that it was a brief encounter.

They hugged again, surprising each other. It was tighter. And warmer. Shauna took it with her, until the cold sank in, and with it, the nightmare.

"Bleedin' ecstasy!" she hissed.

"Seriously?"

Like any good mother, Shauna had warned Sara about drugs, about addiction and the destruction it causes. Sara sat silently, nodding along, while Shauna convinced herself that she had scared Sara off them. That she had done her job.

"How stupid!" she said.

She saw the gardai on regular patrols of the estates. The cars and strangers rolling down their windows, as they passed through. The young boys and girls too, running up and down to them, leaning in to shade the business that was picking up the slack in opportunity.

Where did Sara get the pills? How much were they worth? How much does she owe? Were they for herself? Were they to sell?

Shauna was just about to turn a corner, when she heard the tick-tick-ticking of something metallic, approaching her from behind. She stopped and turned around.

A young boy on a red tricycle pulled up beside her, wearing jeans and a frayed red hoodie with the hood pulled up. He did not look up at Shauna. Or acknowledge her.

Instead, he stood humming a high melody, reaching for each note.

"What are you doing on your own?" she asked.

He stopped.

Wishing that she could take her words back, she watched him push down on a peddle, turn and bolt off. She did not see his face, as he tick-tick-ticked away from the city.

She was shaking her head when she reached the bus stop. There was a bus about to shut its doors. She stepped onto it and lifted up the buggy. The front wheel jammed.

Shauna had to pull and shove it, to free it.

"Maaa!" Melissa cried.

No one helped.

****

With her back pressed against the bus window again, Shauna shifted the buggy's rain cover, just enough to hold

Melissa's hand. The pill was still in her coat pocket. It was the thought of the young boy that was gutting her. She had no idea why he was cycling the streets alone. Or where his parents were. She could have helped him though, if she had been behaving like a proper mother, which was what Shauna aspired to be.

Ever since she had Sara, the looks people gave her implied the opposite. She always seemed to be doing something wrong.

Paul worked in a warehouse, where his wages went up every year, and it never made a difference. They lived with Shauna's parents, who said they did not mind, until Shauna and Paul had their second son on the way.

By then, they had a bit saved.

In 2010, they moved into a house with a council renting plan. It was another 10-minute walk from the flats, with grass in the garden. Shauna had never been happier, which was fortunate, because they could not afford to move.

Now, a mother of four, Shauna could hardly tell where the time had gone. She could tell stories, list dates and times, tastes and fears, and everything else about each of her children. She could name each of them by the sound of their footsteps in the dark, when they came looking for her, after they had a bad dream. No amount of money could buy her that.

All she wanted was to be with them.

Squeezing Melissa's hand, before tucking it under her blanket, Shauna fixed the rain cover, then straightened up. A moment later, her phone buzzed in her coat pocket.

It was her mother, calling to explain that she would be at Shauna's house, waiting with the kettle on. Shauna clutched onto the buggy, fearing she might not make it.

When she hung up, she blinked away her tears.

The bus turned a corner, charging the breath in her lungs. She began to pant as if there were stallions cantering, digging their hooves into her chest. She looked around, sweating again, with her defencelessness unnerving her. She stretched over and rang the bell.

As soon as the bus stopped, she hurried off and took a swig of Melissa's bottle.

Walking up to the top of the road, she reached the place where the flats used to be. She looked up about as high as where she had lived, where she had lingered between the concrete and the stars. Then, her eyes traced a line to where the steps would have been.

To where she had found a baby, when she was Sara's age.

She had snuck out of their flat, without a coat or shoes on; she tip-toed over to the ledge and looked up at the night. Her breath was dangling in front of her, melting like chandeliers of ice, when she heard the tiniest cries coming from the steps.

Rushing over, she found the baby boy. He was in a plastic carrier seat, wrapped in a blue blanket, with a bottle propped on top.

She dropped to her knees, to lean in and look at him.

"Where is your mammy?" she asked.

He stopped crying.

She touched the bottle, which was warm beneath her fingers. Then, she rubbed his chubby cheek, which had toughened against the cold.

Picking him up, she cuddled him.

She fell in love with him that moment. She christened him Alexander Leon, hoping the grand name would provide him with a grander life. She also swore that she would never let anything happen to him. That she would take care of him.

When her mother found them, she called the Gardai, despite Shauna's pleas.

The baby was taken away.

Shauna looked down at Melissa, who had fallen asleep in her buggy, with the sun cracking the grey sky above them, warming the air. Shauna checked the time on her phone.

It was nearly 2pm.

Without another look around, she hurried home, where she stood searching for her keys at the front door. When her mother opened it, Shauna could hear the kettle bubbling.

Sitting at the kitchen table, with Melissa playing by her feet, Shauna explained everything to her mother, who did not flinch. Instead, she reminded Shauna of the time that her mother caught her with a packet of cigarettes. Shauna rolled her eyes.

"Ma," Shauna said. "Am I a good mother?"

Her mother sat solid as a rock. "You are," she answered.

Shauna looked away.

"Do you remember that baby on the steps?" Shauna asked.

"I do," her mother said.

"How could I ever forget?"

The front door opened.

Shauna's sons, Niall and Sean, came running up the hall, fighting to give her a hug. She smiled while the drabs of light that the day had to offer, illuminated the joy in her eyes. Once they pounced on her, squishing her with their love, they took off, over to her mother.

Shauna stood up.

She was going to wait for Sara in her bedroom. The scene of the crime was where she believed her daughter's punishment time should be served.

Sara would be home any minute.

Sitting on Sara's bed, Shauna jumped when the door opened. Sara looked just like her mother did that morning, when she found the pills and rode the bus. She criticised Shauna for going through her stuff, then hugged her and apologised.

She said that the pills belonged to her boyfriend. That she was only supposed to have them for the night. That it was a mistake.

Shauna held her daughter's hand, on the bed that she had finally finished making. She grounded her and took her phone, the pills and the TV from her room.

She would deal with the boyfriend later.

Before she did anything else, she wanted to talk to Sara about her own life. About the dreams and the plans that she had had. And the baby boy that she thought of almost every day.

She was hoping that if Sara knew her better, she would do better.

Wiping her tears, promising she would, Sara went back downstairs to help her grandmother prepare dinner. Shauna sat on the edge of the bed.

Without a clock in the room, she felt the tick of time on her bones. She wondered what was next.

"It's being a mother," Shauna said.

VIII

THE SCIENTIST

6.45 PM THURSDAY, NOVEMBER 3RD

Some people said that it was accepting death. That it was mad to go without a way back. To Luke, it made perfect sense. He was a scientist. Of course, he wanted to go to space. He was a normal nine-year-old earthborn boy when the first clear images from the Hubble telescope were published in *National Geographic* magazine. When he stood on top of a grassy hill, staring up at a clear blue sky, wishing that it was a plaster he could rip off. Like the beginning of most love stories, Luke never looked at the world the same way again.

Growing up in a small Wicklow town, surrounded by fields and forests, there was not much for him to do, other than explore and build worlds of his own. He would return home every evening, believing that the stars were pin pricks in the night, where the light had burst through. What Hubble captured was far more beautiful. Far more destructive too.

There was sheer blackness, glittered with groups of stars that were burning and forming in the colourful gowns of the gases belonging to the nebula. There were cataclysmic explosions, concealed by the unfathomable distance that separated us and them.

Hoping to catch a glimpse of the cosmic catastrophe, Luke stood there all day, trying to reconcile what he saw with what had been discovered. When the sun set on him and his questions, he ran home through the fields to lie awake in his bed, scolding himself for not looking hard enough. From then on, he never accepted anything for what it seemed.

He was a shy boy who sometimes stuttered when he talked to strangers; he panicked while trying to think of something to say. He gave up on the idea of friends, deciding that it was best to stay away, because he did not think it was worth the possible humiliation.

It was his first mistake.

By the time he started secondary school, he was lonely. He had to imagine every kind of adventure on his own, as his mother, father and older siblings had outgrown the curiosity that he possessed. His bedroom walls were covered with every image from Hubble that he could find, continually reminding him that life could ignite at any moment.

He had not even tried to fail.

On his first day, he walked up to a group of boys who spotted him coming and called him 'Lanky'. Without a fluster, he retorted, then discovered that he was surprisingly funny.

Once the nickname and the friends stuck, he was surprised at how easy it was.

Now, looking out at the rows of science students sitting in front of him, he pulled himself back to the present.

"Do you see?" he asked.

There was laughter.

Luke stopped pacing the podium, lifted his hand over his brow to shield his view from the fluorescent lighting that was hung in Lecture Room C. He was the resident astrophysicist at Trinity College, where there were 20 first year students listening to him.

He was giving a talk on failure, which seemed fitting, considering that he was standing in the one place he never believed he would be, filling with the same urgency he felt 20 years ago, when he discovered he did not know what lay beyond the horizon, just that if he had the chance, he would go. With, or without, a way back.

"Take a ten minute break," he said.

The students exited.

****

Resting on the wooden desk beside the podium, Luke dropped his head into the palms of his hands. Frustrated, he reminded himself that dust and gas, floating around in the dark matter of space, gain weight and with it, gravity. Under pressure, the atoms fuse on a nuclear level, irritating themselves iridescent. That is how a star is born. Then, it spends billions of years tearing every volatile piece of itself apart, while humans spend a few marvelling up at it and the others, navigating by them and wishing upon them.

It was a violent, yet vital, part of life. Realising that changed his.

He took a deep breath.

Lifting his head, he pushed himself away from the desk, walked over to the board, picked up a piece of chalk and wrote the word 'possibility' on the greenboard. The door opened and the students returned as he put the chalk back.

"Right," he said. "Where was I?"

Back up on the podium, he rolled up his sleeves and started pacing. He was staring down at his brown leather shoes, scratching his chin, until he clicked his fingers.

In secondary school, Luke made his next big mistake.

He fooled himself into believing that he could make up for the time he lost. He was not thinking about what he wanted to be, when he launched himself into every available subject and sport.

By the time he was 15, he was forging signatures in students' notebooks to earn some pocket-money, while making more friends and gaining more confidence. There was not a cinder of his childhood self left, except that he was excelling in all three of his science classes.

Believing that he needed to be challenged, his parents and teachers agreed that he should skip fourth year. He, however, felt very differently.

He still loved the stars. But for their beauty. Not their behaviour.

Convincing himself that he could capture it, he told his family he wanted to be an artist. And despite the mediocrity of his grades, he fought through his growing frustrations, worked endlessly and compiled a portfolio.

In his final year, he attended an art college open day, where he was blown away by the display of art. Or rather, how little talent for it he had.

It was his first taste of failure. And although it was essential, it was bitter.

Not long after he gave up his dream of becoming an artist, he began to pull himself apart, doubt by doubt, questioning who he really was. How had he wasted so much time?

It was constantly on his mind, even at football practice, when he dove too deep into a tackle, came down on his arm and broke it. He could do nothing with the pain, other than sit with the sinking realisation that it did not hurt as much as what he had been doing to himself.

Then, all he could think of was the stars, battering themselves bright. He knew he had picked the wrong fight when he saw his science grades were still his highest.

He applied to study science at Trinity, where he began class the following autumn. He stood out on the college green, looking up at another clear blue sky, warming with the possibility that he would make it to space. Plenty of people had done it before. Why not him?

He could not stand under the night and name the constellations. But he could explain how they became. That was the thing about science, what most people did not know was the most interesting part.

It was also the greatest failure of all.

"Booooooooo!" the students whined.

Luke stopped and pitched his hand over his brow.

"You're not leaving us!" one of them said.

They laughed.

"Stop it," he said. "We don't have time."

Tomorrow, they had to move on.

****

The question Luke was asked most, worried him most. Death was inevitable. Even for the stars. When they run out of fuel, their core collapses. In less than a second, they no longer resembled what they were. Or the life they had fought for. In a flash, shockwaves are sent shuddering through space, birthing other stars and shattering other solar systems. It is called a supernova. Luke wrote his college thesis on it. Of course, he wanted to see it.

Knowing all there was to know, or rather, all that was known about it, he wanted to get as close as possible, as maybe something had been missed. Maybe he would be the first to see it.

"How could I stay?" he asked.

There was silence.

Luke took it in his stride, turned and walked toward the other end of the podium. His pace was keeping his thoughts straight; reluctant to break it, he carried on.

After graduating, he flew to America to work with NASA. The space agency continually recruited young scientists to aid their research. Anyone in Luke's class could have applied.

There was nothing special about him.

He did not stand out in college. Or in the States. He did not drink tea, coffee, fizzy drinks or juice. He did not have any allergies. Or trouble sleeping.

He was made for space.

When he returned home to the Celtic Tiger, the four months he had spent at NASA aligned him perfectly with an abundance of offers. He was not with the space organisation long enough to learn much but he did grip the ropes that bound his dreams.

It astonished him how easy it was.

Making his next decision was also easy, as Trinity sweetened a Ph.D. in astrophysics with the possibility of using the Hubble telescope. Choking with excitement, he accepted the offer; years later, he did not think he would still be there, talking about failure. But then, as a scientist, he had to make the right amount of mistakes, before he found the right answer. If he was curious enough, he would not give up.

The mistake people made was believing they could not understand. That they were not smart enough. Or even worse, that they were not interested.

"As scientists, we failed." he said.

He stopped, checked the time on his watch. He had 13 minutes left.

Looking at his students, following his every word and movement, he dropped his hands and stood squinting, sweating and running out of breath. The students were on the edge of their seats, despite knowing how the story ended.

In 2012, he was sitting in his small office at Trinity, where he was working as a researcher, while contemplating the different ways he could get to space. During his Ph.D., there had been a call for astronauts. But he did not apply, thinking he was not ready.

Scrolling the internet, he came across an article on the Mars First project, which was an initiative to send people to Mars by televising the trip that had only been completed by rovers and probes. It was a one-way mission, simply because there was no way back.

Luke knew that the technology needed to transport enough fuel for the interplanetary travellers to return had not yet been discovered. That did not bother him.

He did not want to be on TV.

Knowing he was going to apply, he kept putting the application off, wondering how he could stand out. The day it was due, he was working at a summer festival for Trinity. He applied some glitter, found a quiet spot behind a tent and videoed himself detailing the reasons why he would be useful on Mars. Then, all that was left to do was to write 1,000 words on his greatest fear.

Smiling, he wrote, "fear not applicable".

Months later, he was sitting in his office, when he got an email declaring he was one of the one percent. That he should hold his breath.

He had almost made it.

****

Soon after, the questions started. First, the journalists came with their Dictaphones. Then, he was on the radio, realising that he had not told his family, who were happy for him, when he eventually called them. His mother kept every article and recorded every TV interview. Somewhere in the middle of the mayhem, he was asked to give a talk about his journey at the Science Gallery, where he had begun to help curate events. Afterwards, people came up to him, asking him the same questions. How could he go? And why?

Without replying, he changed the subject.

He only had a few weeks to complete the next step of the Mars First programme, which was to pass a medical and psychological evaluation. Luke played football every week and ate well. He did not smoke or drink alcohol. He had nothing to worry about, unless he was mad.

He was speechless when he failed the medical exam.

The doctors did not know what was wrong with him, just as he did not know how much it meant to him. Devastated, he went to different specialists, where he tried every test and got no answers. He was unable to help himself.

It was agony.

Luckily, he broke out in chicken pox and recovered, just in time to pass the medical exam and move onto the next stage, which seemed to be waiting and waiting. As the months passed, he continued to work at the gallery, where the only problem he had was an old one.

"Now," he said, "there is no time."

He used to try and explain what he learnt in college to his family and friends, who never understood a word of the science he spoke. Eventually, he gave up, thinking they did not need to know, once he did. It was a mistake that most scientists made.

Luke had to use his imagination to find new ways to communicate the science that he had studied. Breaking down everything he knew to fit an exhibition or talk, he experimented with the language and descriptions he used.

If his audience left confused, he knew he had not done his job. Nor fulfilled his duty. As a scientist, it was the hardest discovery he ever made.

Over the years, he read and learnt different pieces of information about the Mars First Project. What was most important was that they ran out of funding.

That did not surprise Luke.

His reaction did.

Listening to astronauts describe the effects gravity had on them, never interested him too much. He had imagined the journey too many times, to believe them without experiencing it. But what he could see, after the supernova of his dream, was all that was left: his life spread out like the crashing cosmos, as if he were already floating in space.

"What breaks," he said, "creates."

Stepping down off the podium, to sit on its edge, he

straightened his legs and leaned in towards the students. With his brown eyes looking out at them, he filled with hope.

"Now," he said, "do you see?"

The students drew their breaths, then nodded their heads, packed their bags and left. When the lecture room was empty, Luke zipped up his coat, picked up his briefcase and turned out the lights. He had to go up two flights of stairs before he reached the ground level, crossed the main entrance and stood outside, where the cold, clear night was perfect for stargazing.

Luke kept his eyes on the puddles left by the rain earlier, until a quarreling couple, carrying plastic bags and sleeping bags, caught his attention. Reminding himself it was rude to stare, he looked ahead at a junction, the smoking traffic and the steamy crowds.

All the way to the pub, to play scrabble with his friends, he walked and wondered at what was around him. Knowing there was a ticking clock, echoing deep within the treasure box of life itself, he did not need to look up, as something made from the same stuff as the stars, surely abided by the same rules.

Trust him, he was the scientist.

IX

THE HOMELESS

10.30 PM THURSDAY, NOVEMBER 3RD

There was a purple heart spray-painted onto a north inner city wall. It enclosed the names, Kev and Nina, who were standing beside it, arguing under a streetlamp. There were three plastic bags at their feet, filled with everything they owned, except the spray paint that Kev had stolen earlier, hoping to cheer Nina up. She was due in court for stealing toiletries from a pharmacy; the last thing she needed was a graffitied promise that she could not take back.

Hurling the can of paint down the street, Nina muted the growl grappling through her teeth. Then, she surveyed the clouds gathering to suffocate the stars, scoffed and looked back at Kev, who was leaning toward her, gasping for a word.

"What if the guards come and see us standing beside it?" she said. "Are you thick?"

Kev ducked as if he dodged a punch, turned and took a couple of steps back. Reluctantly reminding himself that they still had to hop a fence before they could go to bed, he checked both ends of the street were clear, walked over to Nina and put his arm around her.

When he tried to kiss her, she turned her cheek.

He walked away.

"Suit yourself," he said. "I won't be long."

At the junction ahead, he turned left, jogged up the path and down the set of stone steps that led to the Royal Canal, where he had stashed a small piece of carpet under the nearby bridge. Waddling alongside the current, he huffed and puffed to himself.

He could understand Nina's point. Not her tone.

He was 23 years old. He was clever in school but bold. It was ADHD, the doctor told him, when it was too late. Kev had already been told too many times that he could do nothing right; he no longer wanted to try. At 16, he left his parents' house, thinking he had figured everything out.

Two years later, he ran out of favours and couches to crash on. The streets were his only option, while drinking and taking whatever drugs he could were all that blunted the edge of the knife that fact held at his throat.

Now, drinking less and using less, there was barely a scrap left of the boy he once was. There was only a belief hardening like cement within him, that he would die out there.

Reaching the bridge, he stopped and took a €20 mobile phone from his pocket. It was the most valuable thing he owned, despite never having the price of credit or anyone to call. He turned on the torch, shone it on a pile of rubbish, smiled and stuck his hand in.

When he retrieved the carpet, he returned to Nina, who was standing as far away from the painted heart as she was willing to walk. Kicking at imaginary stones, she was in her own world, where she could have looked carefree if it were not for the baggage.

Eight years older than Kev, she was slighter and quieter; not a bit of her was built for the life they were living. She was from a nice, well-educated family, who had had everything a child could want, except belief in the stories she told of abuse.

Instead, they blamed her mental health.

They wanted her to take more medication, so she took every other kind than that prescribed, thinking that if they did not believe her, they did not know what was right for her. She walked out of her parents' house two years ago, not knowing where to go or how to get there.

With the change in her pocket, she bought a train ticket to the city, then wandered around until dawn. She was partly blue when the gardai found her asleep on a bench. They took her to the nearest homeless centre, where she woke up.

She never saw herself where she was now, dressed in strangers' clothes, hungry and smelling just like she felt, which was horrible. But she would not go back.

If she had to take her story back, it would kill her.

Kev appeared from the darkness, looking as if he were carrying a sack over his shoulder. Nina crackled to life with laughter, stepped away from the wall, closer to him.

"C'mon," he said. "Not now!"

When he reached her side, she kissed him, surprising him again. He shook it off and looked around. The street was empty. He was ready.

For almost a week, they had been sleeping in a tent that they had hidden in the backyard of a derelict house across the street. Grabbing the bags and rushing over, Kev dropped them beside the front wall, hopped up and threw the carpet over the spiked fence that was guarding the property's perimeter. Once Nina was standing in front of him, he gripped onto the "For Sale" sign, held out his hand and bent down.

"Time to shine, darling," he said.

Nina grabbed onto him without hesitation; she let herself be pulled and boosted up over the fence. Kev passed her the bags, climbed up and removed the carpet.

For the minute it took, they were flawless.

Walking up the overgrown driveway, into the darkness, the inkling of ease, of returning home, rustled over them. They let it prickle their skin, knowing that it would not last long. That they had to take what they could, when they could.

From the street, their torchlight could not be seen.

Neither could their bit of bliss.

****

At the back of the crumbling house, there were mounds of scrap, surrounded by looming shadows that shifted in their sleep. It was hard to believe that Kev and Nina were safer there. Standing hand in hand, they scanned the dark for the discarded door that was concealing their tent. Their torchlight was barely making a dent in the night that had pierced them together. Whether it was the cold or their fear, their legs were trembling, threatening to buckle beneath them.

Finally, Kev found what they were looking for, squeezed Nina's hand and passed her the phone. After showing her where to point the torch, he stepped over the rubbish and got to work. A few minutes and readjustments later, the battered cloth was their paradise again.

"Righ'," he said. "M'Lady, your castle awaits."

Giggling, Nina jumped in.

Kev took a second to savour the syrup of her smile, before making his way, cautiously, to the back wall, where he stood urinating under a tree. Looking up at the stars, he saw prison bars instead of branches, then wondered what he had expected. Why had he even bothered?

There was no shooting star that could solve his problems.

On the streets, wherever they lay their head, they had to defend. They had to sleep with a steel pole or a brick, some sort of weapon that might keep them safe.

The hostels were not much better. There were drugs and thieves everywhere, which made it impossible to stay clean or sleep. Once they were separated into gender specific rooms, they had to fend for themselves. Kev had a lot of experience protecting himself. But Nina was different. He could not leave her and wait for her bruises to tell the story.

Zipping himself up, he shrugged off his thoughts.

Back at the tent, Nina had folded down a corner of their sleeping bag, laid out the book they were reading, alongside a cheese sandwich wrapped in tinfoil. Kev jumped in and kissed her.

When they were tucked in and warm, he picked up their book and began to read. With the wind lashing its whips all around them, they left themselves behind.

Existing only in the pages, in between the lines, they played their favourite characters, revelled in the fictitious dreams, toyed with their hopes and stuck close. It was the moment that Kev and Nina looked forward to most; when they were in it, they were unbreakable.

But they knew nothing lasts.

Nina sat up.

There was enough tobacco in their tin for at least

four cigarettes. She rolled one up, then put the rest away. Ducking under the sleeping bag, she resurfaced at the bottom.

Kev stopped reading, to shine the light on her.

"Are you listening?" he asked.

She nodded and smiled.

She did not realise that her short auburn hair was in tufts. Or that a sprinkling of dirt on her cheeks, resembled fresh freckles beneath her bold brown eyes.

"Ya ride," he said.

He winked.

Without blinking, Nina turned and opened the tent door a couple of inches. Kev shone the dimming torch on the book and continued reading. A moment later, a blazing light filled the tent, slackened and cradled Nina, who was shielding a burning candle wick.

Kev was still and staring, until he leapt and blew the flame out. Collapsing as he let go of his breath, he grabbed Nina, who began to cry. He knew why she poured out her heart every night until she fell asleep, though it did not make it any easier to bear.

He believed everything that she told him, what she lost and how she loses herself when she cannot forget. He understood her mind goes somewhere else. And why she leaves him sometimes for days. But what he believed did not matter, he thought, because he did not.

"It's alri'," he said. "Go to sleep."

Taking the only sleeping tablet they had left from his coat pocket, he gave it to Nina with a dribble of wine. He swallowed the last mouthful, switched off the light and spooned her still. If he had let her go, he would have been the one to shudder.

He had met her outside a hostel a year ago, when they got a bottle of wine together, rather than a bed on their own. They had stayed up the whole night talking, taking cover wherever they could, for as long as they could.

They had been together ever since.

Sharing everything they had, they dared each other to get more, to do better and to laugh as they picked each other up. They fought and made up in the streets because they had no better place to go. No home. No ticket. Nothing more important than what was in front of them.

Kev had been trying to imagine them somewhere else: on a beach or in a house. But he could not. No matter how many books they read to each other, or how many stories Nina concocted, all he saw was the consistency of the concrete in his tomorrows.

Holding her tightly, he drifted in and out of sleep. The city shifted through its gears, while the birds began to sing.

"Wake up!" Nina said. "Kev!"

He opened his eyes as she untangled herself from his arms. She sat up and turned off the phone's alarm. It was six am: four hours before Nina had to be in court.

"Remember," he said, rubbing his eyes, "this is the hardest part."

****

Outside, where it was still dark, the early morning dew was dripping from the backyard like froth. Kev and Nina were wearing almost everything they owned, which meant they could hold hands, leaving the tent, their only comfort, behind. In a slow and solemn stride, they reached the fence and stood silent, trying to time their escape. Without knowing it was safe, they waited until they could no longer stand there, climbed up, took a look and hopped over. That Friday morning, they were lucky. They did not have to run.

Grasping at Nina's hand, Kev nudged her as they passed the spray-painted heart. Nina gripped her plastic bag, pulled up her hood and walked on.

Kev stalled for a second, then kept on going.

By the canal, Nina checked her reflection on the water's edge and said nothing, while stitching herself back into Kev's seams. It was easier for both of them to forget what they had to do next, when they had each other.

At the bridge, they stopped again.

Kev tucked Nina in beside the wall, took the piece of carpet from his shoulder, stepped into the darkness and hid it. Grinning, he returned to Nina's side, picked up the bags, put his arm around her and squeezed her. He never told her about the prayer he said every morning, because she did not need another reason to worry.

Making their way across the city, they shook against each other, fighting the cold and the demons that haunted them. That slithered through the city's corridors, calling them.

They did not lift their heads or loosen their grips, until they were walking alongside the River Liffey. When they set their eyes upon the dawn that was dishing itself out in the sky, serving peaches and cream instead of clouds, neither of them could look away.

The warmth was the closest thing to hope they had felt in a long time. Letting it drip over them, they smiled at each other.

Seizing the last of his strength, Kev hurried up the quays, dragging Nina with him.

"I'm starving," she whined. "Gis a burger."

They laughed.

A few minutes later and out of breath, they arrived at a centre for the homeless, where the smell of toast nearly knocked them out. They sat down and drank two cups of coffee, ate three slices of toast, a bowl of cereal and a banana each.

Afterwards, they went through their pockets and their plastic bags, making a mental note of what supplies they had. They put their phone on charge at the reception, went to the bathroom and freshened up. 15 minutes later, Kev was back sitting at the table, clean shaven and wearing an XL navy shirt. His dirty-blonde hair was smoothed over with water.

Waiting for Nina, he pulled at the collar that hung loose around his neck. He was watching the clock on the wall tick toward 9am: an hour before court.

He hated courts and everything to do with them. Having been in and out of them, he could not help sweating every time he took a step inside one.

Slapping his legs, he straightened up.

"Well," Kev said. "Look at this."

Slapping his legs again, he lit up.

Nina was standing in front of him, wearing a green woolen dress with a black polo neck and trousers. Her hair was brushed behind her ears. Her green beaded earrings were trapping rays of light. Her face was glowing, though her eyes were weary, as she had never learnt to take or believe a compliment.

She slouched over to him, dropped her bag and sat down beside him. Resting her head on his shoulder, she looked around at the other people, eating and chatting, acting like everything was fine. Like they belonged there, just as she did.

"I'm scared," she said. "What if..."

Kev shushed her, then hugged her. Squeezing her with everything he had, he wished she had given him the chance to steal what she needed. He would have committed the crime the second she told him what she wanted.

Now, all he knew was they needed more than a smoke.

"C'mon," he said.

They stood up.

Back on the street, Kev rolled two cigarettes, passed one to Nina, then headed for the court. The sunlight was running its fingers through the clouds, caressing their cheeks and the River Liffey.

Trying to stay close to Nina, Kev avoided the cracks in the pavement for superstition's sake. Nina stayed a step ahead of him, avoiding him.

She had taken a step back inside herself, where Kev could not reach her. He could not stop looking at her either, when they sat down. They shared their last smoke.

But nothing else.

Standing back up, they walked toward the court entrance with their shoulders slumped. Kev jumped a step and grabbed Nina's hand, which was warm as fresh dough, just as the moment she held onto him, before their reflections in the glass doors shattered them.

Kev opened the doors and began to sweat, as Nina let go of his hand.

When she shuffled in, he followed her.

They were red-faced, laced with agitation. By the time they got through security, they were silhouettes of themselves. Moving and shifting from foot to foot, trying to figure out where they had to go, they returned to security, where a silent finger pointed to the top of the staircase, and left them panting and panicking on their arrival.

Spotting the elevator, Kev cried out. Then, he clocked a Garda.

"Garda!" Kev yelled. "Garda!"

Rushing over, unsteady on the shiny floor, Kev halted and asked where Nina had to go. The Garda took a piece of paper from his pocket, looked it over and told Kev that some of the morning's proceedings had been cancelled and rescheduled, including Nina's.

Kev was bitterly confused when the garda repeated himself.

"I heard ya the first time!" Kev yelled.

Back by Nina's side, his words flew from his mouth, so fast and fused with profanity, that it took Nina some time to understand him. Then, she burst with joy.

"C'mon," she said. "Let's go."

Picking up their bags, she grabbed his sleeve, dragged him out of the court and sat him down on a wall around the corner. After rummaging through their bags, she scuttled off and left Kev rocking back and forth, holding his knees, banging his head.

"They don't care what it took," Kev said.

Repeating the words, he was seething, believing everything he had done was for nothing. That he had not made a difference.

Nina arrived back, grinning. Irritating him with her disregard for what had just happened, she hid her hands behind her back.

"Pick one," she said.

He pointed left.

When she revealed her hand, it was empty. Kev groaned

and rolled his eyes, itching with impatience. Nina whipped out her other hand, enclosing their cigarette tin.

Kev looked at it, then down the road.

Nina opened it and held it under his nose. It was full of brand new, smoked cigarette butts that she had picked up off the street. The smell leased Kev a lust for life.

He jumped off the wall, into the sunlight, where he danced around, hugging and kissing Nina, delighting in her success. With enough money for a cheap bottle of wine, or some cider, they would get soup and sandwiches in the evening, when they would trade some brand new, robbed razors for two sleeping tablets. Then, they would celebrate.

If Kev knew their tent and the rest of the rubbish would be thrown in a skip the following morning, he would have stolen something sweet to eat.

"Nooooo!" he yelled. "The phone!"

He was cursing at himself, when Nina smiled at him, reached into his pocket, pulled out the phone and handed it to him. She had collected it earlier, after dressing for court.

Kev kissed her.

Six days later, Nina moved into a rehabilitation centre, leaving Kev alone on the streets. If he knew she had applied, he would not have spray-painted the purple heart on the wall.

He would have spared them that argument.

Interlude Pt. IV

M.A.D.

11.00 AM FRIDAY, NOVEMBER 4TH

Above the Criminal Courts of Justice, the dark shapes of flying birds were swimming through the blue sky. The sun was plating the windows of the surrounding buildings in golden light. I unlocked my bike, while pushing the thought of that morning's cancelled proceedings aside. I cycled away, focusing on the day ahead. The River Liffey was glinting between its stone its banks. The candy-coloured leaves were dropping from the trees, prancing across the street, where they cracked and crunched beneath my wheels, delighting the devil in me.

It was my first day off.

I was going to grab some groceries, head home and put on a wash before calling the people I needed to interview. I was no longer worried about what I had gotten myself into.

I knew exactly what I had to do.

Turning onto O'Connell Street, I took a breath as I felt the weight of the cardboard beds, tucked under every foot of free shelter. I shook my head at the seagulls stuffing their heads into the crammed bins, scavenging the wasted meals, which were enough to feed the begging.

When I reached Parnell Street, I locked my bike and walked to Moore Street, where the stall vendors were yelling in perfect timing, chiming along the cobbles. I smiled with the comfort of knowing somethings never change, even if they do not always look the same.

After buying some meat from the butcher, some fruit and vegetables from a stall, and anything else I needed from the old shopping mall, I returned to my bike. With three bags full of goods hanging from my handlebars, and a backpack full of notes, I steadied myself on the saddle and took off like a paper plane, swinging and swerving all the way to the Royal Canal.

Approaching the bridge, I spotted a group of children playing by the water's edge. Their voices and their laughter were soaring as high as any balloon could go.

I peddled harder and began to climb the road. The handles of the bags beneath my fingers began to tighten and thin; then slip from my grip, rip and spill potatoes, mushrooms and oranges. I pulled the breaks and wobbled to a halt.

Heaving myself and my bike onto the path, frustration and embarrassment scalded my cheeks. The other bags peeled from my fingers, twisting my wrists, forcing me to let go.

I bounced out of the way.

I was trying to compose myself, when I heard a tick-tick-ticking, closing in behind me. I turned around and saw the young boy on his tricycle, holding two oranges.

Handing them to me, he did not say a word.

"Thank you very much," I said.

He did not budge.

"Will you be my girlfriend?" he asked.

I was stunned.

My eyes lunged at my feet, which were steeped in the mess I was in. I looked at him, pleading his decision.

"I am far too old!" I said. "You need…"

But before the words finished leaving my mouth, the boy had reversed and returned to the giggling group of youth. Glancing around to see if anyone had noticed, or knew the boy, I bent down to gather my groceries.

As I lifted up my bike and reassembled the carnage, the young boys and girls whooped and whispered as they hurried back up to the street, striding shoulder-to-shoulder, toward the North Circular Road. The boy was on his tricycle, tick-tick-ticking behind them.

He did not look back.

Carrying myself home, I understood what I had been thinking and feeling, how I had been prepared to throw my hat out of the ring so quickly. I had not been listening to the vibrato that trembled in the tension. Or the diminuendo that illuminated the precious moments and protected the most vulnerable. Or the strumming of heart strings, when love or loss or life takes flight across the ocean of the unknown, spreading its wings willingly.

I had not been listening to the city's symphony. I had been covering my ears with the fear of failing to capture it in its nonsensical, heavenly entirety.

But there was no more time to be scared.

"Not now," I said.

X

THE STALL

11.30 AM FRIDAY, NOVEMBER 4TH

UNDER THE blue and white striped tarp, there were five sold-out trays gaping at Sheila from her stall on Moore Street. That meant it was a good day. So far, there had not been any trouble, though the feeling that it was coming never shifted. With only a handful of stalls remaining, the vendors did not have much say on what happened to them next; the future was hanging over their heads, just like the seagulls diving off the battered bricks to chase the pigeons away from the scraps on the ground. Every day they turned up for work, wondering who would still be there. Who had given up?

"Hey honey," she said.

"Can I help you?"

Stepping onto the pavement, Sheila's blue eyes beamed beneath the loose strands of her blonde hair, blowing wildly in the wind. She did not look like she was ready to walk away because she was not. She had been standing in the same spot, selling fruit and vegetables, for over 40 years. Why should she have to leave? What was she supposed to do?

She adjusted her pink puffer coat, tore a small recyclable bag from the roll stored in her utility belt, smiled and jittered with the same joy she felt every time a customer came along. She was reminded that life was nothing if it was bitter.

The young man approached her, pointing at a tray of mushrooms. Sheila began to discuss the dark pattern that the clouds were knitting above them, while she filled half of the plastic bag in her hand, pinched the top and spun it. When she looked up at him, he thanked her.

"No problem, sweetie," she said.

"That'll be a euro."

The man handed Sheila the money, thanked her again and walked off, smiling and swinging the mushrooms by his side. Sheila put the coin in her belt and zipped it closed.

The street had taught her to keep her eyes open. To know what was happening around her at all times. Otherwise, she would not make a penny.

The first time she stood there, she was eight years old. Her mother had to tap her on the shoulder, reminding her to breathe. That was how scared she was, adrift in the hustle and bustle of what seemed like a different world, when there was only an inch between the stalls and the vendors yelling over each other, charming and haggling for every penny.

What deals they did, they did in silence because there was never enough of the good stuff to go around. But there was plenty of opportunity, which was all they needed.

Sheila was the youngest of six children. If she wanted money, she had to work.

She got into the swing of it quick enough, watching her mother and grandmother working together, moving effortlessly and efficiently, side by side, catching customers like flies in the webs they weaved with their secret recipes and stories. Pressing upon each other gently, sharing unspoken jokes over a few feet of cobbles, they made the world their own.

Sheila sold her first batch of potatoes, by simply holding them, trying to look busy. When an elderly lady asked how much they were, Sheila's mother had put a hand on her shoulder, leaned down and answered for her. Sighing with relief, Sheila handed the potatoes over.

Her hands, soft as whipped cream, were powdered with dirt. They had not been clean since.

"Whatever kindness you give," her mother whispered, "will come back to you tenfold."

Sheila nodded at her mother. But she did not truly understand her words until she ran the stall herself, which was something she never thought she would do.

It was not easy work. Not pretty. Not fancy.

It was honest.

For ten hours, six days a week, she got up at 5 am, went to the market, bought her produce, set up the stall and served her customers as they came. Whether there was rain or hail, or sometimes snow, she was standing there, without any shelter.

A ferocious shout shushed the street.

"What was tha…" Sheila said.

She stalled.

Two men were walking down the path, staggering drunkenly and bickering. They had passed earlier, sober.

Leaning against the stall, Sheila watched them, with the dappled light in her eyes darkening under the creases of her frown. She knew what was going to happen next. She was bracing herself, when one of the men punched the other.

She gripped the stall.

The injured man shuffled away, slowing to a stop opposite Sheila, who looked at him sternly, while placing her hands on her hips. The tall, wobbling man held up his hands, protesting his innocence, just before his friend charged at him, knocking him against the stall.

Stunned, Sheila grabbed a hold of them, reefing them apart.

"All I am trying to do," she screamed, "is a day's work!"

The men landed on the closed shop front opposite her, where they continued to fight. She turned around to mend her display, then realised it was a waste of time.

In the corner of her eye, she spotted a young female garda pull up on a bicycle, speaking into her walkie-talkie. Easing back onto the stall, Sheila was grateful she no longer had to be involved. But if she was asked, she would not step aside, leaving the stall unprotected.

She would never do that.

Once the men saw the garda approaching them, they stopped wrestling. The man who had tried to plead his innocence earlier, punched his friend in the nose and scarpered off.

The other man dropped.

"This has to be a joke," Sheila said. "Where are the cameras?"

The garda looked away.

****

A few minutes later, Sheila was arranging some lemons. She had her back to the handcuffed man, face-down on the pavement, yelling at the Garda, who had been joined by two male colleagues. With the four litres of vodka and two bottles of wine in his backpack, they carried him away, kicking and complaining. Waiting for the street to resume its pace, cleaning the slate, she did not turn back around, until all that was left of the altercation was a few crooked crates and the last nervous shake of her hands.

The other vendors had not taken their eyes off her. They watched her as she inhaled the city's air. And as a smile untied itself from her lips. Then, they got back to business.

She was going to miss them.

They grew up on the street together, trusting and relying on each other. They raised their families and mourned their losses. They would stick together for as long as they could. But they could not blame each other for getting another job, deciding to study or sit on the couch and figure it out. If they could afford to, and were able, Sheila wished them well.

She was too old. Maybe too stubborn.

Scanning the cobbles crammed with empty crisp packets, discarded receipts and other filth, she jiggled as she caught a giggle in her throat. She looked at the stallholder closest to her, whistled and nodded at the coffee shop across the street.

When her friend nodded back, Sheila walked away.

She never believed there would be a day that she would fight tooth and nail for the stall. Or that there would no longer be traders and punters packed wall to wall. But then, she had believed the promises the council made.

She would never do that again.

At 18, she finished school, quit the stall and got a job building dialysis machines for a biomedical company. Learning more and earning more than she ever had, she did not miss the stall. She did help on the weekends, if her mother needed her.

Sheila could not say no.

She met her husband, Ray, at a dance, where they fell in love. There was not much more to the story, other than they had not spent a day apart since.

After giving birth to their first daughter, she left her job and returned to her spot by the stall, where it felt like she had never left. She could not regret her decision because she had never imagined her life any other way.

At least, not until she had to.

Back at the stall, there was a woman with a pram and two children, standing beside three young men, chatting and smoking. Sheila knew their faces from the hours they spent on the street, shifting from one group to the next.

She gave them discounts when they were short. She would help anyone as much as she could. But she had to make a living.

"Hi everyone!" she said.

They did not respond.

Stepping down into her spot in front of the stall, she took out the sandwich she had packed for her lunch and sipped her coffee. The people walking down the path were cutting around the stall, rather than trying to squeeze past.

That was not good business.

Sheila tried to catch the eye of passers-by, while reciting the deals she had on. Nothing she did made a difference, until she let out a shout.

"Come on lads," she said. "Yis have to move!"

Brushing the loose strands of hair off her face, she dug desperately for a smile. The group looked her up and down. The cold wind blew like a brute between them.

She did not budge.

The group shrugged at each other, then moved on.

"Thank you," she said.

She smiled.

She was holding onto a crate either side of her, when the

path cleared. There was a man in a shirt and jeans at the end of the stall, staring at her.

"Why should they move?" he asked.

He folded his arms.

Sheila turned away from him, seeking some peace. She was taking a moment to breathe, when her neighbour winked at her. She let her shoulders sink and the kink in her brow ease.

Turning around, she spent no kindness.

"What?" she asked. "How dare you!"

Stepping back onto the path, she walked toward him without taking her eyes off him. She strained her neck, trying to understand how he could judge her.

"Stand in my shoes," she said. "Then ask why."

With her cheeks a raw red, she clasped both of her hands around her belt. She stood in front of him, stretching all five foot of her.

"Now," she said. "Piss off!"

The man took off, blushing, while the group across the street laughed. Sheila shook her head with frustration, grabbed some loose potatoes and began to bag them.

Reminding herself that the street had changed, not her, she heard a slow tick-tick-ticking creeping along the other side of the stall. She stood still and listened.

With an inkling of what was coming, she looked up.

****

On the tips of her toes, gripping a tray of tomatoes, she tried to catch a glimpse of the opportunist. The tick-tick-ticking ceased, just as a tiny hand, as dirty as hers, felt its way over the top tray of plums. When it tried to steal one, she grabbed it. Gently, but firmly, she guided it toward the end of the stall. Repeating her mother's words, she reached the last crate, where a young boy appeared in front of her, with the hood of his red hoodie pulled up. His blue eyes were like little venturous oceans, pouring over his freckles, breaking against her heart.

"Some things never change," she said.

She smiled.

Squinting her eyes as she assessed him, she let go of his hand, picked up an orange, tossed it and caught it. The boy shuffled into a sturdy stance, without looking away.

Sheila guessed he was about ten years old, too young to be wandering the streets alone. Wondering who was looking for him, she threw the orange to him.

Grabbing it with both hands, he flinched and smiled.

"What vegetable makes you cry?" she asked.

He looked down, considering the question. Finally, he stomped his foot.

"An onion," he answered.

He looked up.

"Exactly," she said. "Next time, you'll get one in the head!"

The boy laughed.

Stuffing the fruit into his pocket, he did not speak before disappearing behind the stall. Sheila peeped and saw the red rusted tricycle he was sitting on.

It tick-tick-ticked, as he sped away.

"Oi," she yelled.

Picking up a plum, she waited for the boy to look at her, then threw it. He stopped and caught it with one hand, took a bite and chewed with a dribbling delight. As he vanished around the corner, away from the city, Sheila picked another plum and ate it.

With the juice rolling down her chin, she thought of her three children sitting by the stall, munching on berries and pretending to work. She could not imagine them as children, walking that street without her at their shoulder.

"How much?" a voice asked behind her.

Sheila jumped.

Turning around, apologising, she served the waiting woman. After adjusting herself and the stall, she traded into the darkness because the streetlight only stretched so far.

The next few hours were spent scuttling up and down her patch of street, bagging her produce and her profit, packing up the rubbish and making lists for the morning. The cold slithered up her sleeve. But she did not shiver.

Last year, the council tried to revoke the stallholders' right to pass on their trading licences to their children. They fought back and won, yet nothing had been done to restore the street or their businesses. Instead, they were made certain of what they had become: the last front in a war they did not ask for.

Sheila knew her children may not want to take over the stall. That they only helped when she needed them. That did not mean they did not deserve the right to their legacy.

She had been standing on the same ground for generations, adapting to the city's changes. She met people from different countries, who requested fruit and vegetables she had never heard of, then used every bit of them, in ways Sheila never imagined. She tasted the world, bagged it and passed on the recipe.

She had regulars from when her mother was alive. That went out of their way to buy from the stall, to remind themselves of the way things were. Some just like to hear the stories she told.

When a light rain began to fall, she packed up the last of her boxes. She knew the clock was ticking toward the end of a story. The others knew it too.

Her husband was waving at her from their van. She waved back, just as a young woman, with long braids in her hair, walked up to her.

"I hear you had some day," the girl said.

Sheila looked at her.

"Don't you worry about that," Sheila replied. "What do you need?"

When the girl handed Sheila a €50 note, she broke it into smaller notes and coins.

"Thank you," the girl said. "And c'mere to me!"

Pulling a leaf from the top of Sheila's head, the girl said goodbye, then walked back up the street to the hair salon where she worked. Sheila laughed to herself, knowing it did not matter what the council built. Or how high they built it. Underneath it, there would always lie the lives that made Moore Street.

Like a diamond buried there, she shone with hope.

Kissing her husband and packing up the van, she headed home to eat the dinner he had prepared and get ready for morning. She did, after all, have a stall to run.

"If you sit down for too long," her mother had said, "you'll never get back up."

XI

THE WEAVE

7.00 PM FRIDAY, NOVEMBER 4TH

DREAM WAS not being superstitious. She was being careful. The two bare bulbs hanging from the low ceiling were simply not dousing the partitioned shop with enough light. That night, she was not taking any chances. Gathering her long braids of hair, twisting and knotting them on the top of her head, she threaded lightly, over the cracked tiles, avoiding the shadows that were circling her. Along their edges danced the collectors of a curse that was uttered a long time ago, far, far, away, from Moore Street.

She had too much to lose, to turn her back on it.

Searching the overloaded worktops lining both sides of The Shine beauty salon, Dream found a lamp. She dangled over piles of curlers, scissors and pins to pick it up. Smiling, victoriously, she carried it back to her mother's beauty station, plugged it in and turned it on.

When it made no difference, she rolled her cocoa eyes.

"At least," she said, "I tried."

With a client due at 7pm, she cleared her mother's workspace. Consisting of a steel table, a mirror and two wooden chairs, it did not exactly scream with the glamour

Dream had imagined for herself. But it was a place to start.

She was 20 and studying business management in college. She had been borrowing her mother's space in the evenings, with the hope she would have her own by the end of the year. It made no sense to her, to make money for someone else.

Picking up the pink suitcase filled with her equipment, she placed it on one of the chairs and opened it. Folded on top, there was a piece of black and orange cloth.

Dream pinched a corner and lifted it up, letting the pattern of floral plumes unfurl before her. The fabric was woven in West Africa, where she was born.

Spreading it out over the table, she flattened it down by running her fingers over the intricacies. The rolling threads reminded her of home, where she would sit out on the balcony, in her mother's lap, plaiting her hair and ignoring the sun setting over the African sky; where she would divide, crisscross and repeat, until she fell asleep.

If she closed her eyes, her fingers would finish her weave. There was no reason for the incremental beating of her heart. Or her sweaty palms.

"Why," she asked herself, "are you so nervous?"

Pulling a chair closer, she sat down, reached into the suitcase, removed a cardboard box and gently placed it on her lap. When she opened it, she smiled down at the yellow tea-set that was inside, painted with blue birds. It was the most precious thing she owned.

It belonged to her grandmother, who was one of the first women in her family to travel the world, to settle in Italy and export perfumes and other luxuries to Africa.

By the age of 24, she was an entrepreneur.

She moved back to Africa, when she met Dream's grandfather. She built a mansion with stone lions and guards at the gate, started a family and hired some help.

Dream's grandmother was too busy to cook.

Dream laid out the cups and saucers, teapot and spoons, just as her grandmother had when they used to sit in her gold-tipped garden, drinking fruit tea. Holding the pot and pouring, her grandmother would tell her stories about the places she had been. How she did it all for herself.

All by herself.

Looking down at her watch, Dream shook herself up. With ten minutes left, she took the blonde hair extensions for her client, draped them over her black jeans, picked one up and began to brush it. Outside, the wind was sweeping the rain against the glass door, though it was the colour of the sand, caught in the wind's mouth as it whistled down the dirt paths she used to walk to school, that was occupying her mind, unnerving her.

It was not safe there.

In the dark, amongst the snakes, lurked men that would kidnap her and chop her up, eat her body parts and bury her bones. Her father and uncles had told her about the dangers that awaited her, figuring that she had to know what to expect, to protect herself.

A lot of children died on their way to school. And in other ways too.

"Voodoo," she whispered.

Her eyes darted around the room, then peeped through the shop's partition, into the mobile phone repair shop on the other side, where the guy on duty was looking at his phone, suspecting nothing. Reminding herself she was in Dublin, she took a breath.

All she ever wanted was a room with a view. To look down and see how far she had come. To wake up every morning, charging toward the sun.

Earlier that day, she went to view an apartment with her boyfriend, Kash. Both thought it was better than she imagined, so they left an application with the letting agent, who said he would call Kash with an answer that night. Dream would have to finish the weave, before hearing what he had to say.

As a child, she did not know the difference between light and dark. Or that there was a choice. She was too young to pick a side. To understand poverty, death or religion.

She loved her parents unconditionally.

Her father was from a poor family. He grew up in a shelter built from scrap, practicing Juju and worshipping the Devil. As the eldest of six children, he was expected to provide for his family and not the rich Christian girl he had fallen in love with, despite knowing that it would never work.

That it was against tradition.

In the beginning, Dream's parents did not believe they were cursed. They married and moved into a house her grandmother bought them, opened a grocery shop in the front room and had Dream. When they had her brother, the Devil came into play.

Her father's family fed her baby brother a parasite, committing him to a life that would end at 19. But Dream did not know the meaning of evil, until she asked her mother, a year later, why she was not poisoned. Why did she get to live?

"You are a girl," her mother said. "Girls do not carry the family name."

The door burst open.

****

For a moment, the rain fell like crystal spears on the welcome mat. Dream was mesmerised by its wrath, until she told herself to keep her head out of the dark. Jumping up, she greeted her client, Hannah, took her coat and her umbrella, showed her to the bathroom and turned on the kettle. Back at the beauty station, she checked her phone. There was no message from Kash. She filled with doubt, wondering what could go wrong? What stood in their way?

She placed a hand on her grandmother's blanket, unwilling to give in easily.

"It's not the time," she whispered.

"Or the place."

Looking herself over in the mirror, she wiped her brow and rolled up her sleeves. She tied back two loose braids of hair, then reapplied the red stain to her lips.

She was not glamorous because she did not want to be. She liked the dark cherry that her cheeks churned when she laughed too much. Or when she was embarrassed.

She wanted to make other people feel beautiful. No matter where they came from. Or how much they had.

They deserved to matter.

Hearing the bathroom door close, she picked up the tea pot, filled it with the kettle, put it back and pulled out a chair for Hannah, who strutted out of the shadows in a skinny pink dress, with her blonde hair swooshing over her shoulders. Dream whistled at her as she approached.

Hannah twirled and sat down, noticing the steam rising from the teapot. She looked at Dream and smiled with approval.

"This is lovely," Hannah said. "This too…"

Holding the corner of Dream's blanket between two of her fingers, Hannah caressed the pattern. Dream gathered the tools she needed, while a shiver of excitement tickled her pride. She thanked Hannah. Then, she wrapped a towel around her shoulders and got to work.

With her hands moving methodically through Hannah's hair, pinning it and brushing it, Dream listened to her talk about her life, her fears and her faults, unable to hold back her own. Filled with compliments for each other, there was not a second of silence.

"Isn't it funny," Dream said. "We're never happy?"

Outside, the rain was unrelenting. Dream checked her watch: it was eight o'clock, which meant she did not have a lot of time. The shop closed at nine.

"Right," Dream said. "I have to stop talking!"

Hannah laughed.

Pulling her chair closer, Dream did not utter another word. She began the last plait, while Hannah scrolled through her phone.

Dream eased into a rhythm, whenever she weaved hair. She did not notice the time go by. Instead, she travelled through it in her mind, to all the memories entwined, crisscrossing and repeating. To where the curse always lurked.

By the time she was eight years old, her mother was pregnant with her fourth child. The food in their shop was perishing because she had no time to sell it.

Dream's father was no help.

He was drinking more and more, disappearing for days and throwing fists when he came home. The curse was taking its toll.

In a fit of fear, her mother decided to follow her older sister to Ireland, where she could earn more and create a new life for them. Dream did not believe her, until two weeks later, when she left; Dream thought it was a nightmare she would wake up from.

Even when she was preparing the meals and tidying the house, she hoped her mother would walk through the door. But all she did was phone, as often as she could.

For her siblings' sake, Dream turned off her emotions.

Three months later, her brother died.

Her father told her the parasite had taken him younger than most. That it was best not to tell her mother, who was due to give birth any day.

By then, none of it made sense to Dream.

She thought it best to believe her father. To spend her time looking after her younger sister, braiding her hair and playing with her. Each day, they would savour the sunsets, seared into the horizon, and hold on dearly to the last reaching finger of light.

For two years, Dream's father lied to her mother. He told her their son was in hospital, while drinking the money she sent over. He rarely bought food, paid the electricity bill, came home or checked on them. Dream knew something was wrong.

Sitting on the couch, too afraid to sleep because they had no money to turn on the lights, Dream and her sister clung to each other and prayed. With no way of knowing where she was supposed to go, or how she was supposed to protect her sister, Dream cried until daylight christened their window again. Then, she got them both ready for school.

On their way, she found enough change to call her mother. Two weeks later, they arrived in Dublin.

"Ow!" Hannah exclaimed.

Dream stopped.

The pin she was using to sew in the first hair extension had slipped through the braid, poking Hannah in the head. Dream put everything down on the table.

"I am so, so sorry," Dream said. "Wait!"

Standing up, she walked away, refilled the kettle and waited for it to boil. Growing impatient as it took longer than she expected, she returned to Hannah.

She was shaking her hands, trying to calm down.

"What is going on?" Hannah said. "Tell me!"

Patting Dream's seat, Hannah turned to face her. Dream put down the teapot, took her seat and looked at her watch. Reckoning that she had enough time for a sup, she got back up, filled the pot and poured two cups of tea.

Then, she spoke about her dream.

"You're not cursed," Hannah said. "You're blessed – just look at yourself."

Not knowing what to say, Dream regretted getting so comfortable. She placed both of her hands on Hannah's shoulders and squeezed them.

"Right," she said. "Let's go!"

Without pricking Hannah again, Dream finished the weave. And after brushing Hannah's hair, it looked like it had grown three inches.

Hannah was delighted. Dream was relieved.

Blushing and gushing over her new hair, Hannah thanked and paid Dream, swearing she would be back, before picking up her umbrella and saying goodnight. When Dream was alone, she fanned herself with her cash and began to dance around, celebrating her success.

It was not much. But it was a step.

She packed up her stuff.

****

It was 9pm. Time to go. The lamp was back where it belonged. Dream was sitting in one of the steel chairs, with her pink suitcase packed and upright, waiting to be wheeled away.

The guy next door was locking up the store. Every minute or so, he peered in. Dream was tapping her foot, acting as if she could not see him. As if everything was fine. Inside, her nerves were thrashing just like the rain against glass panes.

"Where is he?" she whispered.

She laughed.

She was being ridiculous. Kash would not leave her. Especially on a night like that. He had to be late. Or maybe, he was lost. Maybe, it was the curse.

In 2000, Dream's mother met her and her sister at Dublin airport. Dream did not have much to say on the way to their one-bedroom apartment: she was numb.

Then, she met her younger brother.

Knowing that his resemblance to his older brother was a blessing, she could not stop crying. Or hugging and kissing him.

Maybe there was a better life ahead.

When her mother arrived in Ireland, she could only stay with her sister for so long. With too much pride to ask for help, she ended up sleeping on the streets, where she went into labour, surrounded by strangers who did not help.

An angel in a fancy black car stopped, picked her up, drove her to the hospital and paid for her care. He did not leave a name or a number.

"If he was not an angel… what was he?" her mother asked.

Dream looked down at her watch. It was five minutes

past nine. The guy next door banged on the steel frame of the partition, frightening her.

She spun around and looked at him.

"Five minutes," she said. "Please?"

He looked away as she began to scratch at her knees. Stopping herself, she stuck her fingers into her bun, to unwrap her braids from the knot she had spun.

Then, she took a breath.

In primary school, she was bullied about her accent, her clothes and the dark colour of her skin. She hated it, until she learnt how to give it back.

She had grown up beside the jungle. What was she so scared of?

She began to stick up for herself, and anyone else that needed her help. Once, the other kids realised she was no different, they made fun of something else.

On more than a few occasions, Dream had been left sitting, just as she was that night, wondering if someone was coming to get her. Her mother was working as much as she could, while minding Dream's younger siblings: she could not always make it in time to collect Dream from school. The teachers would wait with Dream, then drop her home.

Eventually, Dream was taken away.

Devastated, she moved in and out of 17 different foster homes, unable to settle because she was too far from her family. Or because the people were not nice.

She was not making it easy either. She would sit in the corner of her room, holding her legs against her chest, yelling until she was alone. Rocking back and forth, she would pretend the streetlights were tribal fires, burning to light the way home.

The only consistency in her life was school, as no matter how many times she moved house and family, she remained there with her friends. By the time she was in secondary school, she was popular.

Everybody knew her by her bountiful voice complimenting them. Or calling them out in the halls. Even the Polish, the Spanish, the Romanians and the others began to socialise more.

Kash was two years above her. From West Africa too.

She knew she wanted to be with him because she wanted to tell him everything. She trusted him more than anyone.

He was her home.

"Come on," she whispered.

She stood up.

The guy next door peered through the partition, held up his watch and tapped it at Dream. She looked over at him with her arms held up.

The door finally flung open.

"I'm sorry," Kash said. "I'm sorry."

He was dripping wet, holding a sagging bunch of flowers. Smiling down at her, he reached a long arm out and pulled her close. Welling up at him, Dream nudged him.

"What's wrong?" he said. "You were dancing around, flashing your cash when I walked by!"

Dream pushed him away.

"We got it!" he said.

She kissed him.

He had gone to meet the landlord, to pay their first month's rent and deposit, before collecting her. He wanted to surprise her. Not scare her.

Since she turned 18, she had been living with him in his

student accommodation. They had been working and saving for that moment, for too long.

But the view, Dream knew, was worth it.

Grabbing the handle of the suitcase and his umbrella, Kash stuck out his elbow for Dream to latch on. Then, they stepped out into the rain.

The drops that caught her cheek reminded her of the first time it rained on her in Africa. It was the day before she left for Ireland. And the most beautiful thing she had ever felt.

As she walked into the night with Kash, the streetlight stretched across the puddles, keeping them a step ahead of the dark. Dream did not look back. Or worry about the curse biting her heels.

She was paving her own path.

Interlude Pt. V

M.A.D.

9.25 PM FRIDAY, NOVEMBER 4TH

Earlier that evening, dark clouds had marched through the sky, blitzing the people and the paths with torrential rain. The tirade had not ceased since. Across the road from my house, the Tolka River was sloshing and swelling. I was standing by my beaten window, watching the hopeless pieces of myself sink to the bottom of its battered basin, letting the wrath of the hail replace them. I reached over and ran my fingers along the keys of my piano, startling the silence.

I had not practiced or played in a long time. No wonder I was out of tune.

Turning and facing my bedroom – the antique writing desk, the crammed bookcase, the picture frames and the foot of space to manoeuvre around my bed – I smiled and closed the curtains, knowing that I had never really fled from my purpose. That the darkness crippling me was not seeping from within me: it was descending upon all of us.

"It's time to come back to life," I said.

A second later, my phone rang on my bed. I picked it up and saw the call was from the soldier, Dom, who I had been trying to contact all day.

When I answered, he told me that he was taking shelter from the rain. That I could ask him anything I wanted. I thanked him and opened my notebook, while he began to talk about the night he had had. I sat on the edge of my bed, without looking down at the questions I had penned. I listened to his story, which was filled with feelings of inadequacy, regret and longing. Then, I began to talk about myself.

"You tell other people's stories," he said, "because you don't want to tell your own."

I jumped up.

"I have to go," I said.

He laughed down the phone.

"You're running," he said. "But it's ok: I've been running too."

Thanking him again, I promised that I would speak to him soon, hung up and picked up my black leather boots, put them on and tied my yellow laces. I had planned to meet my friends for a few drinks and forget the week: nothing was going to stop me.

I grabbed my keys, coat and notebook, froze and put the notebook back down. I always brought it with me, so I was always ready to take a dip inside this book.

Standing in the hallway, I examined myself in the mirror, fixed the lapels on my long black coat and pulled up the red hood on my hoodie. I looked myself dead in the eyes, wondering if they would keep my lie, if someone would notice that I was struggling.

I put on my backpack and picked up an umbrella, unlocked the front door and leaned back as the wind assaulted me. I thundered through the puddles and skipped across the roads, with the dull taxi lights passing me by. I crossed the Tolka River, turned and walked by the flats.

When I reached the end of the street, I glanced over at the park. The trees were sagging with nightmares dripping like tears from the branches. I saw a group of young teenagers, chatting and cheering, taking cover under the leaves.

Then, I saw the tricycle.

Scanning the troop, I spotted the shortest shadow and found the young boy staring at me, until his eyes met mine and he looked up at the older boys and girls. I lurched forward, hoping that he would look at me again. That I could rectify that morning.

But I was out of luck.

Sipping a cold, hardy breath, I faced North Strand and set off down the sopping, twinkling path, trusting that nothing could scare me more than sacrificing everything I had worked so hard for. Or forgetting that music lies in the noise we make.

Amongst the triumphs, mistakes and heartache, there is a melody surging blood to skin to spirit, singing in sweet harmony with the spatter of stars that make us. There are verses and choruses of life assembling choirs and orchestras in our names. There is rhythm in our choices, heralding the band to play or sit still.

There is a beating will.

In the morning, I would wake up with a banging head. And a tune so shrill that it would carry the cadavers from their dusty beds, into the rising sun.

XII

THE SOLDIER

10.00 PM FRIDAY, NOVEMBER 4TH

Throughout the entire evening, Dom was a gentleman. He opened the door and pulled out the chairs at the restaurant. He unfolded his napkin and laid it out on his lap. He even used the correct cutlery. He could have pretended to be a different person if he wanted. Nobody knew what he had done. Or where he had been. There was nothing stopping him from enjoying his first date in over a decade, except the regret he could not wash off his skin.

As soon as he settled the bill, he tipped and thanked the waitress. He held the door for his date, used his coat to protect her from the rain, walked her home and kissed her goodnight.

Then, he tore off into hail, with his old ticks itching his bones. He reached the Royal Canal.

Charging over the bridge, he took shelter in the park, where he stood at the end of a path drowned in darkness. He was soaked from the rain and the strain of wondering how nobody could tell he did not belong, when he took out a cigarette and sparked it.

"What was I thinking?" he asked himself.

"Why did I bother?"

It did not matter who he became. Or where he went. The price of his past would always have to be paid; doused in that shade, he could not see a way of escaping it.

Lifting his head, he peered into the park that was poking out of the night. The dogs barking and branches cracking were snapping at his nerves. He pulled on his cigarette, quick and hard, before dropping it and squashing it with his black leather boot.

What did he have to do for a bit of peace? It was not cheap. He knew that.

He stepped out of the dark with his eyes shooting daggers in every direction. He walked over to the canal, leaned over the wall to spit and check his reflection in the swelling water. The raindrops shooting by his head were raiding the surface, distorting his view and silencing his mind. He hung onto the moment, as long as his wits would allow.

Back inside the shadows, he pulled his wet Armani coat away from his dry Armani jumper. He ran his hands over his gelled black hair, while the pale steeliness of his skin strengthened the slice of his stare and the hard line of his jaw.

His greying edges were sharp as razors.

He did not look bad for 45, he thought, he almost looked sophisticated, like he had something to say that was worth hearing – until he smiled, revealing a missing bottom tooth. Pressing his back against the wall, he waited for the rain to stop.

The bones he broke many years ago ached in the cold, though he did not grimace or groan. The only comfort he needed to know was that he could still throw a punch.

Growing up in a block of flats, not too different or far from the ones nearby, he had learnt how to stand up for himself when he was six years old. He was playing on the street, when a boy punched him in the face. Dom ran home nursing his cheek, to meet his father standing at the door, handing him a hurling stick, telling him to sort the boy out.

If Dom did not, he would take the beating. What was Dom doing?

Running away?

Clutching the hurling stick, Dom made his way down to the street, thinking he could not do what his father wanted him to. Then, he saw the boy.

"It was easy," Dom said.

"Surprisingly."

The boy never spoke to Dom again. But Dom did not care. By the age of ten, he had not run from another fight. He had begun to like the fear his fists inspired.

He was no good at school. He could not focus, so he did not stay away from trouble long enough for anyone to notice. The only subject he enjoyed was art.

Sitting in the alley behind the flats, staring down at the fancy art set his mother had saved up for, he did not concern himself with who was watching. He was basking in the thrill of his unbeaten glory, when an older fella came from behind and stood on the paintbrushes, smashing them into pieces. Walking off laughing, the boy did not look back.

Sometimes, Dom wished he had.

He did not understand the anger that lightened his head as his blood fled to flank the fury in his heart, leaving his mind and body cold enough to get it back. Grabbing a brick from the rubble behind him, he picked himself up like a sword drawn for war.

Once he was behind the boy, he started pounding.

Unrelenting, he got his blood.

His hands were trembling, dripping with the stuff, when he abandoned the brick. He sprinted home and told his father, who told him to shower and wait in his room, quietly.

An hour later, the boy's family came knocking.

The boy was a bully, which meant they knew that the beating was coming. That life around there had to take its cut. They just wanted Dom and his father to know that they knew.

Dom had been looking over his shoulder ever since.

Glancing around the park, he could not tell who was looking or lurking. He could only hope he was out of sight. He did not belong there either.

The rain was fading into the wind, whisking the sounds of the city. Dom pushed himself away from the fence and took out his box of cigarettes. The drabs of light reaching across the canal, filled the bellies of the red rubies in his rings. He smiled down at them, trusting that they looked just as good as they were for protection.

In that same second, he heard a tick-tick-ticking.

Spinning around, he leaned into the dark. His knuckles and rings were ready, when a young boy appeared on a tricycle, pulling to a halt.

The tick-tick-ticking stopped.

Dom scoffed.

The boy set his eyes on Dom, while whipping off his hood and nodding. His freckled face was stern as he strangled the sensitivities of his youth.

Dom nodded back, shook by the look of him.

"Do you want weed?" the boy asked.

Reeling back, Dom reminded himself to have patience, then thought that it must be a set up.

"G'wan!" Dom said. "Get outta here!"

The boy puffed out his chest.

"What about on tick?" he said.

Impressing himself, he smiled and gripped the handlebars of his tricycle. Dom took a step back, struggling to believe the boy, who could only have been about ten years old, had just offered him tick: a few days or a week to pay for the weed.

Dom took out a cigarette and pointed it at the boy, who looked down and noticed the black swallow tattooed on Dom's hand, with the joy dropping from his face like a dead bird from a tree. Shifting on his feet, the boy steadied himself on the seat of his tricycle.

"That's a mistake," Dom said. "Always get your money first, never a day or a week late."

The boy shot him a look of disgust.

"You…" he said, "can fuck off!"

Pushing past Dom, the boy peddled through the puddles, along the canal, singing the notes of a song. Dom closed his eyes.

"Oi!" he yelled.

The boy stopped.

"You be careful!" Dom shouted.

The boy pulled up his hood, without looking back. He pushed down on his peddle and tick-tick-ticked away, disappearing in the dark.

****

Lighting the cigarette in his hand, Dom took a long drag. The boy's face was weighing on him, reminding him of how it all went wrong. He pulled at his collar, scratched at his neck, squirmed and dropped his cigarette. Cursing and kicking the dirt, he walked back up the path, to the park gate, where the scars he had from existing on the brink, calloused his face with caution. He inspected the street, hoping he would not see the boy.

Where was he going? What was he doing?

Dom was wise enough to assume he did not have any drugs on him. That he was just testing his own tenacity. Dom would have warned him, told him that the money was not worth it, if he did not already know the trouble that would cause.

He was an outsider too.

Stepping into the light, he made his way to the entrance of a housing estate, with the rain running down his face. He took one more look around, then cracked each of his knuckles, put his head down and kept going.

When he was 14 years old, his mother was pregnant with his youngest sister, Sophie. His family moved to a house outside the city, beside another block of flats, where nobody knew Dom or liked strangers.

A week later, he had taken a beating.

His father was a carpenter, who was drinking too much and too often. He came home one night stinking of whiskey and swinging a frying pan at Dom's mother, who scrubbed whatever she could for a few quid. Everyone respected her for it.

Dom had given up the fighting, knowing he had gone too far. That he could not take back a drop of blood. Or trust himself.

Looking at his father, he could not trust him either.

He leapt from the cloak of his childhood, pushed his mother out of the way and pinned his father to the cooker. His father grabbed him and wobbled, toppling them both and breaking both of Dom's legs. Dom screamed until the ambulance came.

Then, he was drugged out of it for days.

A month later, his father was done apologising. He came home, screaming at Dom's mother to go and get her "little bastard child".

Dom pretended to be asleep.

He did not let his mother, or the man he had just discovered to be his stepfather, know that he knew the truth. Instead, he decided to find his real father, as soon as his legs healed.

Hobbling up to the boys who had beaten him, Dom asked for some real pills and a job. He reckoned selling drugs had to be easier than sitting at home where he did not belong.

He was sleeping on whatever couch he fell on, while selling hash, then ecstasy, once he realised that the Es were more profitable and easier to sell. He was dabbling in his own product too.

All the boys were.

Together, they snorted their first lines of cocaine and scaled the walls to drop acid and hallucinatory bombs on top of the city. Sweating and panting, they roared out in hunger, in belief that there was more to the world than what was on offer.

Crashing and burning, they died together the next day. They reminisced and resurrected, before getting back to work. Dom was no longer peddling around the outskirts.

He was a soldier.

A year later, he got a phone call from his uncle in prison, who claimed to have what Dom wanted. The following day, Dom was in Mountjoy, with a pen and paper he did not need because he already knew his real father.

He was a friend of the family.

He had gotten Dom's mother and another woman pregnant at the same time. Dom's mother told the man she would be fine; she would raise Dom on her own.

His father was a tall, dapper man, who went from selling a lot of heroin, and making a lot of money from it, to injecting it and being broke. Dom did not believe it until he saw him, festering in his own flesh.

He did see a lot of himself in the cut of his father's features. But he could not understand his choices. Dom swore he would not make the same mistakes.

Reaching the end of the estate, Dom stalled and scanned the bus stop. When he was certain he knew none of the other passengers, he dashed over and paid his fare.

Upstairs, he sat down the back and sank into the seat. Rolling his collar down, he rested his fingers on his sister's name, Sophie, tattooed to the bone, sighed and took out his phone.

With a bent thumb, he bashed the buttons and messaged his son. "See you in the morning," Dom wrote.

Pressing his head against the window, Dom looked out at the night whizzing by. His son, Ben, finished school last year. He got a job in a deli and started training as a boxer.

He was just like his father. Except smarter.

At 18, Dom thought he had it made. He was living in a bedsit, with more cash and more product than ever before. He had a girlfriend too, who he left for Ben's mother, Sinead.

Travelling back and forth to London, he was selling the same product for a different set of friends, borrowing from his stash, taking a yoke or two and clubbing with Sinead. He was not keeping track of himself. Or the money.

In London, he got the call, informing him his father had a heart attack and died. Dom was not surprised. He knew his father was sick from his habit.

It was the reason Dom did not visit. He could not face the taut tragedy his father threatened him with. But he did make it home for the funeral.

Afterwards, he was walking to his mother's house, when two men dressed in military gear put a sack over his head, threw him in a van and drove him to a field, where they stood him up and held a gun to the side of his head. He could not see their faces under their balaclavas.

"What are you bleedin' playin' at?" they asked.

They fired.

Dom thought he was dead, then deaf, until he heard a voice over the ringing in his ears.

"Too bad you can't thank your father," it said. "His last words saved your life."

Waking up that night, on the green outside his mother's house, he lugged himself over to the front door and knocked. A minute later, his mother met him with tears in her black eyes.

Dom looked past her, down the hall, at his stepfather's silhouette, staggering against the stained yellow glass in the kitchen door. Slipping by his mother, into the dark, Dom's head lightened as his fist tightened.

The next day, he could remember nothing other than the blood.

Jumping up, Dom pressed the button. His stop was just ahead. He ran down the stairs, eyed the street and hopped off.

Close to his mother's house, his phone began to ring. Grunting, he took it out.

It was 11 o'clock.

Sinead was calling to say that the Gardai had been to the door, accusing Ben of fighting in the street. Dom had to talk to his son.

He hung up.

Breathless and buckling beneath the weight of his forfeited fate, he did not know what he was supposed to say. What could he say?

His hands were far from clean.

****

Upstairs in his bedroom, Dom shut the door quietly. The walls around him were bare, except for a samurai sword on a shelf beside a picture of his three children. He shot over to his single bed, sat on the edge and reached underneath. Retrieving a small wooden box, he placed it on his lap, opened and closed it, then put it aside. There was enough for one joint inside. Dom kept it there, like a crutch, knowing one puff would make everything better.

He had not touched a drug in over a decade. Instead, he hopped walls to get away from the tit-for-tat, knowing he did not want to try this or that.

He wanted his life back.

Staring out his window onto the green, at the suspended cameras and clouds, he gripped his knees.

"What are you doing to yourself?" he asked.

He shook his head.

Too many of his family and friends were dead for the wrong reasons; reasons that were not worth death but could only be rectified by death. Dom did not want his son wearing the same chain of names around his neck.

He deserved better.

The day after Dom buried his father, he moved into a flat in London with Sinead. He could not look at himself. Or get the blood off his hands. He started taking more and more of his own product, while swapping it for others and buying whatever he had heard was good.

He was dragging himself around, like a match that would not light, when he bought some heroin. He injected Sinead and saw a kind of peace that he had never felt, wash over her.

Then, he injected himself and laughed as his troubles dissolved.

"It was good," Dom said.

"Too good."

They were only taking it a couple of times a week when Sinead found she was pregnant. They quit the heroin and returned to Dublin.

A few days later, they were in his mother's house, when his ex-girlfriend called to tell him he had a two-year-old daughter. He was a father.

In bed that night, everything he was and thought he would be, blistered out of him. He was sweating and scratching, crawling out of the bed, to the green, where he dropped to his knees with the toll of time bearing down on him.

In the morning, he got up and went looking for every job and pill that could fill his pockets and his voids. The years that followed were wracked with highs and lows, arguments, prison, missed birthdays and blow.

He should have known what was coming.

Taking out a smoke, he stood up.

Outside, he pressed his back against the pebble-dashed wall. The hairs on his neck prickled. The sirens and stolen cars screeched off in the distance.

Dom lit the smoke.

The second time he went to jail for possession, he did six months. Sinead gave birth to Ben. His mother kicked his step-father out. His youngest sister, Sophie, got sick.

By the time Dom was released, he was no longer afraid to live because of the expectations he could not fulfil. He had been faced with four walls and the fact that he had become what he was running from.

He was not going back.

Dropping his cigarette butt in the drain, he drew a breath of fresh air, then tiptoed back upstairs, picked up the wooden box on his bed and opened it. He took out the small brown block of hash, crept into the bathroom, wrapped it in tissue and flushed it, in preparation for the rainy days to come.

Once he was tucked up in bed, he turned off his lamp and stared at the dark, counting the seconds until he could leave to meet Ben. The first time Dom held his son, he imagined everything he could be, with his father by his side; it kept him clean.

His uncle was out of prison and running a security business. He gave Dom a job.

Dom spent all his time with his family, working or searching for Sophie, who was using more than Dom ever had. She was all skin, sores, bones and smiles, whenever he saw her. She never asked for anything, other than to talk.

Three years later, she overdosed.

Dom went back to the only way he knew how to deal with the pain. Three years after that, he was in prison again. Sinead left him. And he could not blame her.

Sitting with his life falling through his hands like sand in the hourglass, he realised it did not matter if he had a fancy house, car or business; if he was not alive, all that would matter were things he had missed and why. He was not going to die like that.

He got out of prison, went back to work and avoided any reminders of his old habits. He gardened with his mother. He fixed up an old BMW. He answered every time his children called. He told them he loved them.

Tossing and turning all night long, Dom barely slept.

In the morning, he dressed and left the house without saying a word to his mother. He crossed the green, thinking of the young boy on his tricycle, singing his heart out.

"What a night," he said. "What a bleedin' life."

He laughed.

Under a sunny, partly cloudy sky, the wind blew the dead leaves down the path. Dom felt its cold, bitter blade shave the warmth from his skin, cutting and carving so deep that it reached the flesh of his regret. For that second, he let his wounds bleed afresh, knowing he had to stitch them closed, to forget; to be the father he promised himself he would be, he had to forgive himself.

His son was waiting.

XIII

THE FIREMAN

4.30 PM SATURDAY, NOVEMBER 5TH

THE SUN was shining in from the garden, where the flowers and the swing were swaying in the wind. There were floral prints on the kitchen towels and the tablecloth. There was tea brewing in an old pot. The sharp rose-petal scent of perfume was floating through the room. Stuey was gazing out the window, sinking into the sizzle of what lay ahead. Maybe three people shot dead. A suicide. Another parent after harming their child. A hit-and-run. A cat stuck in a tree. Stuey never knew what it would be.

Life is not like a movie. It is like a box of chocolates.

"Do you want to talk about it?" his mother asked.

Stuey sat up, straddling his senses. He reached over and squeezed her hand.

"No," he said. "Thanks Mam."

Her beaming eyes and matching smile calmed his mind.

"Then, get outta here," she said. "Sure, you're already there."

Tilting his head, Stuey drew back his hand, stood up and walked over to the sink, to pour himself a glass of water. Gulping it down, he gasped and wiped his mouth.

His mother hurried over to him, reached up and hugged him.

Standing at 6'2, Stuey bent down and clung to her. Once he had straightened up, stretched and said goodbye, he stepped into the hall that had housed his first imaginary inferno. He reached the sitting room, where he had revived his toys, stalled and stared at the pictures hanging on the wall.

First, he saw his grandfather in his firefighter uniform. Then, he found his father in a gold frame, standing in the garden, smiling under the sun.

Raising a hand, Stuey saluted them.

He was three years old when his father, who was a plumber, died from a heart attack. Stuey was too young to remember much about him, so he learnt every story he heard about him, word for word. He even knew a few about his grandfather too.

Stuey was no soft touch. He was not religious or easily scared. But there were way too many times he should have ended up dead.

Maybe someone, his father or grandfather, was somewhere looking after him.

Leaving the house and the sentiments behind, Stuey took out his keys and unlocked the shiny new fire-car parked on the road. Covered in reflective stripes, stickered numbers and sirens, it was packed with every bit of safety kit Stuey could fit.

As an officer of the Dublin Fire Brigade, he had to be prepared for any situation, at any time. He had to drop everything, even the moments that meant the most.

If he was too late, there was nothing he could do.

Inside the car, he turned on the ignition, reversed and drove out of the tidy estate, past the mowed lawns and window bouquets. Running a hand over his shaved head, scraping his chewed nails against the spikes of his strawberry-coloured hair, he pressed on the accelerator, sealing himself to the seat, driving toward some sort of doom.

Growing up, it was his dream to be a fireman. He might have been a garda or a soldier, if it did not work out; all he promised himself was the flashing lights and the chance to save lives. He was not someone who messed around. Or wasted time.

He stayed out of trouble, studied and hung out with friends who dreamt of making a difference. He had to work too.

His mother had three jobs, plus Stuey and his two older brothers and sister. She could not afford to give them everything they wanted. Instead, she taught them how to get it for themselves. She raised them, all by herself, to be their own heroes.

Descending the road to the training centre, Stuey glanced through the shedding trees. Across the green, he could see the redbrick building, the gothic tower and arch, the army of windows and the black tiled tips, paving paths to the clouds.

Raising his chin, he tightened his grip on the steering wheel.

At 18, he was studying for a degree in engineering, knowing that he could not sit around, hoping and praying for his opportunity. To satisfy his ambitions, he tried martial arts, dancing and paying attention in class. But he always felt he was in the wrong place.

It ate away at him, until five years, three applications and a year of welding later, when he finally got the job of his dreams. What he knew now, would not have changed a thing.

Indicating, he turned into the centre, drove through the iron gate and up the small winding road that led to his other home. Parked in his spot, he unbuckled, pushed himself back and took a deep breath.

"Showtime," he said.

He was not scared of death. It was the only certainty in life. There was no reason to worry about it twice.

It was the living that unnerved him: they could hurt him. Sometimes, they could even make him doubt his choice.

Smothering his sensibilities, Stuey stepped from the car and strode across the ground, nodding at his colleagues, who were dressed in their navy uniforms, chatting by the firetrucks and ambulances. The legacy roasting the air around them sparked the buzz that lit the blood in their veins. Stuey inhaled, simmering into his role.

Through the heavy doors and long corridors, he checked his phone. He had no messages or missed calls, nor time to let the disappointment, trickling down his throat, linger for long. He was not in the position, or the place, to have his emotions get in the way.

As soon as he reached the dressing room, he changed into his uniform and boots, tightened his belt and walked up the stairs to his office. He shoved his regret back in his pocket, along with his phone. Greeting his fellow officer, he sat down at the desk and scanned the pages in front of him. Then, he laughed and joked.

When he was alone, hunched over the desk, he did not break a sweat. He delved into what he had missed since yesterday, completed some paperwork and checked his roster. A while later, he looked at his watch, picked up his clipboard and charged back downstairs.

There was only a minute until the bell tolled six o'clock.

Outside, in the yard, the station crew were gathered. Stuey made his way to the frontline, stopped and saluted them. He knew every one of the men and women, their families, their fears and their dreams. He knew what each of them had been through, what they had lost and what lived in the darker parts of them, haunting them.

But most importantly, he knew what he was asking them to do.

Going through the memos, courses available and updates, he assigned their numbers to roles, while they stood close to each other. He did not stutter, or look in any other direction, as he asked them to risk their lives.

"Fall out!" he ordered.

They dispersed.

****

First, a call comes through to the control room. The information and the address are entered into the computer system. The predetermined response is selected. The nearest resources are located. Then, the officer hits a button and the bells ring at the station. The printers start printing. The computer screens light up. Within four minutes, the team has to be gone. There is no room for error. No time for doubt.

The third incoming call snapped Stuey out of his contemplation. He was standing beside the firetruck, D33. His crew were already inside, seated and belted, peering out the windows, pointing at him and their watches. Stuey rolled his eyes and jumped in.

Patting the driver on the shoulder, he turned around, winked at the others and hit a switch beside him. The sirens blared. The whole team whooped.

Stuey faced the road, with his heart beating harder than a hammer, nailing him to the seat, just like it always did. For those few minutes, he did not know what was coming, what bitter treat had been plucked from the tray of life's salty, sprinkled horrors.

All he knew was that a car was burning on a city street. Sometimes it was accidental. Other times it was for an insurance payout or a warning. Or it was just some kids with nothing to do and nowhere to go. Whatever the reason, Stuey told the driver to speed up.

It took him over two years to become a fully qualified firefighter and paramedic. There were sessions on dealing with the trauma he would face but there was nothing that could have prepared him for the screams, the decapitations, the heat of the blaze or the blame.

He was too young.

He was swept out of the classroom into the furnace, without blinking or really thinking. He met his girlfriend, Leanne, who was a teacher, and just as committed to helping others as him. Somehow, she made him nervous.

Two years later, they married.

They bought a house close to where Stuey grew up, had two daughters and date nights. They were happy for the first few years. They were on each other's side.

Up ahead, there was smoke swimming over the rooftops, into the darkening night.

"Right," Stuey said. "Are yis ready lads?"

The blue flashing lights, bouncing off the bungalow windows, detailed the determination on their faces.

"Yes Sir!" they replied.

Swinging around a corner, the driver slowed and beeped at the small crowd of spectators blocking their way. Stuey sharpened his frame and leaned forward, staring at the car that was burning under a streetlight, like it had just been driven straight from hell.

An hour later, he had completed the incident report. His team was back inside D33. The car was black and hollow. The crowd had gotten bored and closed their doors.

Stuey picked up the radio, declared D33 available, hung up and sat back. Another call came in before he had put his seatbelt on. He rolled down his window and bit his nails.

Four minutes later, D33 was where it needed to be. There was a young man, slumped over on a step, unconscious.

Stuey and his team got him grumbling, while they waited for an ambulance to arrive and transport him to A&E. After filing the report, he declared D33 available.

The next call came in as soon as he hung up.

It was half-past ten.

Once again, Stuey and his team were on the scene within a couple of minutes. They were parked by the Royal Canal, where a man had been stabbed in the leg.

Waiting for another ambulance, the team managed the man's wound and kept him alert. He was bleeding heavily, talking and slurring, telling the team that he had just come from a flat, where he had been smoking crack, when he regretfully decided to rob the wrong house.

"What were the chances?" he asked.

His head dropped.

Stuey took out his phone, scrolled the screen, then put it away. Hoping for a message from his daughters or his wife, he heard a whizzing behind him.

He shot around and looked down at the Royal Canal.

BANG! Bang! Bang.

He threw his gaze down the path, where there was a smoking bin. Then, he noticed a young boy, staggering toward the edge of the canal, covering his ears with his hands.

A second later, he disappeared.

Sprinting across the concrete, Stuey stopped by the trees, with the shadow of their seasonal striptease suckling on the steel toes of his boots. He took a step back and eyed the empty path, wondering how fast the boy could possibly run.

When he reached the charred bin, he spotted a red tricycle beside it.

"Little shit," he said.

Shaking his head, he walked over to the edge of the canal. He glared into the water that revealed nothing, other than the nightmares he knew to have drifted through it.

The chopped-up body parts. The broken-latched briefcases. The unfortunate swimmers. The washed weapons and slippers. No wonder he thought about ending it all.

How could he turn off?

Sirens filled the air.

****

Back at D33, the ambulance team arrived. Stuey welcomed the medical crew, checked the report, signed off and waited for the blue flashing lights to depart. All that was left of the incident were the bubbles of blood, popping on the pavement. Taking one final look at the canal, where everything seemed as it should, Stuey questioned whether he had ever believed such a thing, before climbing into D33 and putting on his seatbelt.

"Anyone for a cup of tea?" he asked.

His team cheered.

Speeding toward the training centre, he imagined the boy parking his tricycle by the canal, lighting the banger and throwing it in the bin. He must have been too young to understand that he was standing too close. Or to know what was left after the smoke.

To be fair, none of them did.

Every day, Stuey picks up the pain people inflict on themselves and each other. He listens to their threats and dodges their spit, their stones and their complaints about paying his wages. He sees young boys and girls diving in with their eyes closed, trying to rule worlds they do not belong in. He always meets them again, one way or another.

Three years ago, his wife left him.

He had just been promoted. Everything was looking up. Except him. He could not leave all the damage and death behind him, bagged and tagged at the scene.

He was either arguing with his wife or hiding behind extra shifts at work, where he found some peace knowing he was always ready to save the day. He did not talk about the debt he felt he owed. Or the tragedies he faced.

Instead, he moved into his own place and saw his daughters a few times a week. He could not speak to his wife because he could not look her or the person he had become in the eye.

He began to think he should have been the one that died.

Diving into the depths of his despair, he did not phone or show up to work for three days. He sat sleeplessly in the dark, waiting for something to change, to cave the dirt on his premature grave. Then, there was a knock on the door.

It was late afternoon.

Stuey did not open the curtains, until he peeped out and saw his boss looking back at him. He opened the door and excused the mess, before sitting down and listening to his officer, who did not need to ask what was wrong, as they both knew that Stuey was not alone.

They all had their own battles to fight.

Heeding the gothic spikes poking the horizon, Stuey sat up and smiled. He was alive and healthy. He never drank or smoked. He had two beautiful daughters, a job he loved and colleagues that had become his family.

What more did he need?

Up the winding road, parked outside the station, Stuey ensured D33 was available and ready, jumped out and guzzled the air. The night sky was clear above him.

The stars were in their places.

Stuey entered the station, unable to deny his hunger. He grabbed a seat and sat down at the dingy table, where he and his team cracked jokes about the job, and the silence that often followed, often said more.

"When are you seeing the girls?" a colleague asked.

Stuey took a bite of his sandwich.

"Monday," he replied.

Wishing it was true, he changed the subject. He had not heard from his girls or his wife. But he knew he could talk to his crew if he needed to.

He trusted them with his life.

The bell rang!

Stuey and his team grabbed their gear and ran to D33. The call was a domestic fire, with another firetruck and an ambulance already at the scene.

Five minutes later, all Stuey could see was a smouldering glow through the windows on the second floor. The building was old, just like the others beside it.

The flames were spreading.

Working together, the men and women of the Dublin Fire Brigade saved every tenant crammed into the place, bunk by bunk. They cornered the fire, put it out and filed the appropriate paperwork, all before the birds woke up. Slapping each other on the back, they said their goodbyes, got in their trucks and headed to their stations, to throw water on their faces.

By nine o'clock, Sunday morning, Stuey had received three more calls and filed more reports. His head was heavy, though his green eyes, puffy and red, were yet to dull.

Looking forward to going home, he saw the bridge over the Royal Canal.

"Pull over there," he said. "Please."

Nodding, the driver slowed and parked at the curb.

"A little further," Stuey said.

The driver inched onto the bridge.

"There," Stuey said.

Leaning out the window, he saw the morning sun, sugar-coating the canal. The charred bin opposite it, was no longer smoking.

The tricycle was gone.

"Little shit," Stuey said.

He laughed.

****

Back at the station, the team due to take over were already prepping the other vehicles in the yard. Stuey and his team thanked them, before heading inside to grab their things and make their way home. Banging on the dressing room door, without the energy to say goodbye, Stuey trudged up the stairs to his office, signed over his shift and double-checked his lists. Then, he nodded at his fellow officer and bowed out of the room.

He was crossing the yard to his fire-car when he took out his phone. He stopped and looked around, as if there was someone he wanted to thank.

"See you tomorrow, Dad," his daughters' message said.

Not knowing what to do with himself, or the joy he felt, he kept on walking, acknowledging his comrades. Finally, he reached his fire-car.

Hopping in and locking the doors, he sat and read the message again and again. He started the engine and tore off, with his face hurting from smiling.

He was gliding down the motorway, admiring the shimmering silver and gold that was weaving through the horizon, when the car ahead of him swerved and slammed into the steel barrier. Stuey switched onto alert, flicked on the sirens and called control.

A moment later, there was an explosion.

Speeding toward the flames, Stuey thought of his daughters and his wife, expecting his call. His mother sitting at the kitchen table, proud of what he had become. His father standing in the garden, with the wind reminding the flowers to dance.

His colleagues who had passed.

Without a doubt, he knew he was supposed to be there, pulling up and pouncing towards the danger he was trained to tame. He leapt out of the car, while the driver collapsed in his seat.

The car's engine was hissing. The gaskets were bursting.

Stuey opened the boot of his car, put on his fire-coat and gloves, rushed over to the vehicle and pulled the door handle.

The driver slid down.

Unbuckling his seatbelt, Stuey grabbed and dragged him as fast and as far as he could. Then, the car exploded again, spitting cinders of rubber and metal.

A few minutes later, the firetruck arrived.

Stuey sat with the driver in his arms until the team were by his side, lifting them both up and carrying the injured man away. Patting himself down, checking for burns and blisters, Stuey felt an arm on his shoulder.

His girlfriend, Mel, was standing behind him, in her firefighter uniform. She was gazing at him, with her warm apple pie eyes. She winked and ran at the fire.

Looking back, she blew him a kiss.

"My husband!" a woman yelled. "Matt! Matt!"

Spinning around, Stuey caught sight of a woman charging at the scene. He grabbed hold of her sleeve, stopped her and waved at the officer, just as she collapsed in his arms.

Stuey spotted her car parked beside his.

"Don't worry," he said, "Your husband will be fine."

She cried.

"I was just talking to him!" she said. "We live two miles away!"

Stuey helped her up.

"Thank you," she added.

Turning his head and facing her, Stuey saw the reason why he did not quit. Why he risked everything.

The officer approached, then took the woman's arm. Stuey remained in the same spot, gathering himself and his thoughts, before returning to his fire-car, buckling up and speeding off. The sirens were ringing, seizing the air.

The fire had been put out.

Driving toward the home he shared with Mel, Stuey smiled with the promise of tomorrow. He put his foot down.

"I'm out there, in the grit and the shit, trying to save a life, or bring a life into this world, because I want to be," he said.

"It was my dream."

Interlude Pt. VI

M.A.D.

2.15 PM SUNDAY, NOVEMBER 6TH

Sitting by the Royal Canal, I stared up at the leaves trembling on the branches of the tree I was resting my back on. The sunlight was gleaming through their oranges and yellows, engraving their veins in shadows. I closed my eyes and saw their blue effervescent lines etched onto my eyelids. I felt the heat of the rays singeing away the last of my fear, like I was kneeling at the foot of an altar, peering up at the stained-glass hands of faith, swearing I would not let the darkness escape, even if I had drag it by tooth and nail, into the light.

It was not going to be an easy fight. But I would not look away. Not like others.

I picked up my notebook and flicked through the pages, smiling at the lines of conversation that I had written down. When I reached the beginning, I ran my index finger – tattooed with a dagger to remind me to use my words with precision – under the first lines.

"I was never young," it said.

"But I am not yet old."

Picturing the bonfire scrapping beyond the bend in the canal, I smelt the smoke and the mothers' and aunt's perfumes, dangling amongst the crowd that was singing and searing themselves into the night sky. I remembered why they were all there.

They had never given up.

The alarm on my phone rang, telling me it was time to go to work. I tucked my notebook into my backpack, ensuring I had packed all of my uniform. I stood up and picked up my bike, dusted myself off and walked toward Ballybough.

Admiring the community around me, I smiled at the banners and bunting, the potted plants and plastic candles adorning the window ledges. I heard the scuttle and screech of children playing in the streets nearby. I caught sight of a bicycle wheelie, tearing over the bridge ahead, while I passed two young men, sitting on foldout chairs and fishing.

They were each drinking a bottle of beer and laughing as they discussed the beautiful view that they had been blessed with. I suppressed my giddy delight, wishing I could join them.

Then, my phone rang.

Stopping and searching my backpack, I found it and answered. It was my mother calling to check how I was feeling: if I had reconsidered my notions of quitting.

I assured her that I had.

"Good," she said.

We both laughed.

Once I hung up, I pushed my bike up the bridge and hurried across the empty road. I lifted my bike onto the pavement, bashed my ankle off the peddle and dropped my phone.

Crying out in pain, I felt the burning gaze of eyes on me. I looked over at the path leading down to the canal and saw the young boy standing with a plastic ball in his hands, staring at me. His tricycle was parked at the bottom of the bridge, where there were two boys smaller than him, marking their side of an imaginary court.

I was searching for the right words, when the boy nodded at me, resuscitating the wonder that I had lost. That gripped the trapeze of my heart. That began to swing and somersault.

I nodded back.

"Ready, set, go!" he shouted.

And as he returned to his friends, he let go of the ball and dribbled it on the pavement. Pitching the perfect cadence, he unleashed the thrill of brass in their lungs.

I picked up my phone, hearing the bowing of strings in the hum of cars passing. The snap of percussion in the doors slamming. The sprinkling of piano keys in the laughter and chatter.

Bouncing onto the saddle of my bike, I spun the peddle and took off with the thought of the work I did that morning – all of the notes, interviews and transcriptions I had gone through – firing the metal beneath my feet. Every time I blinked, I saw each of the people I had met and the depths I had reached, gasping for a piece of mind or bit of belief, and continuing to ask questions, to pursue the meaning beyond words and facts.

At the top of O'Connell Street, I pulled up and walked my bike up the hill to the hotel, knowing that there was nothing that could stop me. Except me.

Inside the hotel, I changed into my uniform, rushed back up to reception and checked myself in the mirror hanging above the lounge fireplace. I fixed my scarf, making sure I looked the part, while recognising the spark within me could have torched the dried potpourri that had been facing the desk longer than I had.

But I did not mention my story. Nor my feelings.

ABOUT THE AUTHOR

Maeve A. Devoy is the author of *The Tell Tale Collection*. She studied at Dublin City University, where she received a b.a. in Journalism and an m.a. in Literary Journalism. When she is not writing or interviewing people from all different walks of life, she is teaching creative writing, playing piano and walking her nanny's dog.

Her goal is to create understanding by providing a variety of perspectives and painting as many stories as she possibly can. She also hopes to shatter stereotypes and give a voice to those who have not been heard, so make sure you keep your eyes on her.

I greeted the guests and carried their suitcases, poured their drinks and organised their trips, until they were busy enough for me to shrink behind the computer screen, open the file I had hidden and start all over again because I was no longer the same. I had changed.

And so had the file's name.

"A City Symphony," I whispered.

With the carousels of life crooning and clashing beyond the door, I readied my fingers over the keyboard, trusting that the night had lit the city up like an arena, enclosing the streets and the people queuing to perform. The ticking clocks had already been tossed out the windows, along with the sanctity of sense. There was only a myriad of madness left; dancing and kissing, brawling and crawling, breathing melody into the hearts that were playing dead.

As I said, what you have read no longer exists.

ACKNOWLEDGEMENTS

First, I would like to thank the people who gave me their time, who shared their stories and their lives with me. Without them, it would not have been possible to write this book.

It also would not have been possible without the support of my mother, who has been my side, year after year, reading the many, many versions of my stories and listening to me cry and celebrate.

My father's belief in me meant everything, especially on the rainy days.

My brothers' strength and courage kept my head up and my heart fighting back, even when I was certain that I had nothing more to give.

I owe my sanity to Lisa Keegan, who edited and proofed this book with the understanding of a true poet and a true friend. I will forever live for the moments we sit, imagining new and old worlds.

To my friends, who know I love them and thank them for having the patience to bear me and my dream, I would be lost without you.

I am beyond grateful for each and everyone of you.

Coming soon…

The Maddening
by Maeve A. Devoy